Remembering
The Great War

*In Gloucestershire
& Herefordshire*

Remembering
The Great War
In Gloucestershire
& Herefordshire

Ray Westlake

BREWIN BOOKS

First published by Brewin Books Ltd,
Doric House, 56 Alcester Road, Studley,
Warwickshire B80 7LG in 2002.
www.brewinbooks.com

ISBN 1 85858 226 1

A Cataloguing in Publication Record
for this title is available from
the British Library.

Typeset in Bembo
Printed in Great Britain
by SupaPrint (Redditch) Limited.
www.supaprint.com

CONTENTS

Church of the Holy Innocents, Highnam, Gloucestershire

INTRODUCTION

Just how many war memorials exist in Britain's cities, towns and villages can only be estimated. The National Inventory of War Memorials when they began their task some ten years ago putting forward a figure of possibly sixty thousand. This – thanks to the overwhelming response by volunteers around the country to the Inventory's request to gather and send in information – must surely by now have been reassessed in an upward direction. Even in a small county like Gwent (Monmouthshire) I personally have managed to record over six hundred (see my two books – *War Graves and Memorials in Gwent Volumes 1 and 2* – Wharncliffe, 2001, 2002).

To the final figure, what ever it turns out to be, we must add war graves. These, just as on the battlefields of France, Flanders and other theatres of war, standing (it is hoped) as lasting memorials to those that laid down their lives. Yes – we have them in Britain too. Many wounded soldiers making it as far back as a UK war hospital – only to die from their wounds later – others to lose their lives while in training before going overseas. But – thanks to records kept by the Commonwealth War Graves Commission – we have accurate figures for these: one thousand, five hundred and ninety-three for Gloucestershire (these in two hundred and seventeen cemeteries and churchyards), two hundred and twenty-eight (one hundred cemeteries and churchyards) in Herefordshire.

Therefore from the above, it must now appear obvious that this little book has made no attempt at completeness. Indeed many fine books (and they appear now almost on a weekly basis) have been published dealing with the fallen of just a single, or group, of villages.

The small *selection* made here is exactly that. The stories told have not been chosen especially for their interest, or the memorials for their elegance – every war grave, every memorial, is as important as the next in as much as the name(s) on them must never be forgotten – and all, because of what they represent, can be considered as average.

To those in the areas covered, I invite you (assuming you have not yet done so) to look at your memorials in a new light. It is hoped that I have been able to add something to what is already known. And to those of you passing through these fine towns and villages, take now a little longer over your visit perhaps, and stop off for a while to consider the contribution made by the men, women and regiments of both counties.

As for the geographical scope of this booklet; well a glance at a map will clearly show that the parts of Herefordshire and Gloucestershire covered are those within a comfortable distance from my home near Newport, South Wales. But it is hoped that additional volumes will follow. These going further afield in Herefordshire, and in the case of Gloucestershire, through to the boundary with Worcestershire, before turning to move south-west again and down the other side of the Severn. And yes, I have included a few places, latter Avon or even now North Somerset, but once (certainly in 1914-1918) Gloucestershire. And off course Bristol. A County Borough in its own right for many years, but certainly - if its contribution to the Gloucestershire Regiment alone is to be considered - well within the scope of this work.

ABBEYDORE - HEREFORDSHIRE

St. Mary's

Originally a Cistercian monastery founded in 1147, St. Mary's (Dore Abbey) lies on the B4347 close to the Monmouthshire border and River Dore. This road leading off from the A465, about eleven miles south-west of Hereford. Having walked through the lychgate, turn to find the first of two memorials commemorating local landowner and business man, Richard Crawshay Bailey Partridge. On a plaque attached to a cross-beam the, and it must be said, strangely worded dedication: "Erected to the memory of Capt. R.C.B. Partridge M.C., C.deG. killed in action Sept. 28, 1918 by friends in South Wales." Chairman of the family company since the death of his father in 1909, Richard Partridge also had interests in Pontypool where many local people were employed in the collieries and steel works.

Inside the church at its east end, Richard Partridge is again remembered - this time in the form of a fine window dedicated by his mother (Mary), brother Henry, and sisters. Featuring the figure of King Richard I ("Lionhearted"), and a scene from his 1191 Crusade to the Holy Land, the window also includes the arms of the Partridge family and crest of the Shropshire Yeomanry. The latter being three "loggerheads" (or leopards' faces).

Richard Partridge's military career extended back to the Boer War. Both he and his brother (Reginald) serving in South Africa with the Shropshire Yeomanry and leaving England with its First Contingent on 2 February, 1900. Just over seven months later Reginald Partridge would be dead - killed during a skirmish with the Boers on 29 September.

In September, 1914, Richard Partridge took a temporary commission with his regiment, but, it would appear, did not sail for Egypt with the 1/1st Shropshire Yeomanry on 4 March, 1916. The *Monthly Army List* for this time showing him as being posted to the 2nd Regiment which remained at home. By March, 1917, however, Richard Partridge is given as "attached" to the 7th Battalion, King's Shropshire Light Infantry, then, in the following December, as having been posted to that regiment's 10th Battalion. The 10th, as it was, being formed from the Shropshire and Cheshire Yeomanries – both at that time serving in Palestine.

Friends in South Wales remember Richard Partridge with a lychgate at St. Mary's, Abbeydore.

Having moved to France (the 10th KSLI arrived there in May, 1918) Captain Partridge would gain both the Military Cross and French *Croix de Guerre* before his subsequent death near Havrincourt Wood on 28 September, 1918. Ironically eighteen years, almost to the day, after that of his brother, and exactly four years from the date (28 September, 1914) of his first commission. Captain Partridge is buried at Beaumetz Cross Roads Cemetery, France.

From The Green, Bacton (just a mile north of Abbeydore) the Partridge family worshiped at St. Faith's. The village church where further memorials can be seen featuring in true colour; regimental badges, crests and medal ribbons. There is also a framed photograph of Captain Partridge.

The first of two parish memorials within the church (another window) is situated close to that commemorating Captain Partridge. A stone plaque below noting that it was dedicated by parishioners and friends, and listing (along with ranks and dates of death) the names of seven men that lost their lives.

About 3.30 am on 4 August, 1916, rifle fire was heard to the south-west of a series of five outposts then being held by the 1/1st Herefordshire Regiment close to Romani - the battalion had seen service at Gallipoli and moved from there to

Egypt in December, 1915. The Battle of Romani had began, and at 5.30 four or five aeroplanes flew over and dropped approximately one hundred and sixty bombs on the Hereford's "No.6 Post". Here Private William Charles Mutlow, a farmhand from Cockyard north-east of Abbeydore, would be among the garrison of some one hundred and fifty.

Records note that the morning aerial attack caused no British casualties. Later on, however, a heavy and continuous bombardment by the enemy's six-inch guns left the Herefords with losses totalling thirteen killed and twenty-six wounded - a large number of the men being buried alive. No less than eighty-nine craters were later found in the area within the wire confines of the Post. Charles Mutlow is buried at Kantara War Memorial Cemetery, Egypt.

Timber taken from HMS Britannia at St. Mary's, Abbeydore.

Horace Hughes (the second of two members of the Herefordshire Regiment to be killed) was twenty-three and came from Kerry's Gate Farm - just north-east of Abbeydore. Private Hughes met his death during the 26 March, 1917 attack on Ali Muntar - the Herefords now in Palestine and engaged in operations towards Gaza.

In reserve at first, the battalion was later ordered forward at 1.12 pm to assist the 5th Royal Welsh Fusiliers then held-up by fire from the enemy's position at Green Hill. The advance, notes one observer, was carried out "....with the regularity and coolness of a manoeuvre...." but having established a firing line about five hundred yards from Ali Muntar, all progress was stopped due to heavy machine gun and rifle fire. Relieved from the area next day, the Hereford's casualties totalled two hundred and thirty-five killed, wounded and missing - one of the seventeen killed being Horace Hughes. His body never found, Horace's name was subsequently placed on the Jerusalem Memorial to those who fell in Egypt and Palestine and who have no known graves.

Also with no known grave is Private George Watkins of the 7th King's Shropshire Light Infantry who was thirty-two when he died on 22 March, 1918 – the 1918 Somme offensive having began the day before. Eight o'clock that morning saw the 7th KSLI ordered forward to reserve trenches in the Hindenburg Line west of Héninel – a journey that saw considerable casualties among the battalion. When relieved next day, some eighty men had been lost due to gas and high-explosive shells – among them Private Watkins who is commemorated on the Arras Memorial to the missing at Faubourg-d'Amiens Cemetery.

Thanks to local historians Bob and Jenny Davies, much is known of Thomas Frederick Ruck. The son of John and Ellen Ruck, of Cwm Farm, Abbeydore, Tom joined his brother Percy in New Zealand about 1912. Short, with brown hair, grey eyes and a dark complexion (notes his military records) Tom enlisted in 1916 and was subsequently killed on 30 March, 1918 while serving in France with the 4th New Zealand Rifle Brigade.

The *Official History of the Great War* (Military Operations) records that on 28 March, 1918 the 3rd New Zealand Brigade (this including all four battalions of the NZRB) not only kept off the enemy, but while defending Rossignol Wood improved their positions and strengthened their line by a series of short advances. Two days later Lance-Corporal Ruck would be killed by a sniper's bullet. Tom's name can also be seen on the New Zealand Memorial at Grevillers, just west of Bapaume.

On 26 August, 1918 (the opening day of the "Battle of the Scarpe") the principle task of the 4th Canadian Brigade was the capture of Guémappe. This being south of a spur running south from the ridge of Monchy-le-Preux. Part of the 4th Brigade was twenty-one-year-old Lance-Corporal Herbert William Williams's unit, the 19th (1st Central Ontario Regiment) Canadian Expeditionary Force. Raised and mobilized in Toronto on 19 October, 1914, this battalion had sailed for England on the following 13 May.

In action again on 28 August (the date of Herbert's death) the 19th CEF led the day's attack – this time towards the heavily defended village of Cagnicourt. The going was good at first, notes one observer, but checked by uncut wire and fire from strongly held trenches, the assault was held up after about one thousand yards. Herbert Williams is buried in Quebec Cemetery near Arras.

Although recorded on the memorial tablet as William H. Watkins, the Commonwealth War Graves Commission give Driver Watkins's second name as John. This thirty-year-old recruit dying from pneumonia just three weeks after joining the 60th Reserve Brigade, Royal Field Artillery. Passing away on

21 February, 1917 at the 2nd Scottish General Hospital, Edinburgh, his body was later brought home and buried in the churchyard at St. Mary's. Bob and Jenny Davies record that the Watkins family lived at Hollingwood [close to Abbeydore] and that William was married to Gladys of Pentwyn, Bacton.

Moving back now to the west end, and south entrance to the church, we find there in the crossing the second parish memorial. This time in the form of a triptych located to the left of a fine oak screen by John Abel. Together with its Second World War counterpart (to the right of the screen), this type of memorial is of a kind made by Hughes Bockow and Co. Ltd. using timber taken from the cadet training ship HMS *Britannia*. On this occasion the names of those that served (in addition to those killed) during the First World War have been recorded - these being shown, together with year of enlistment, in gold lettering on both doors.

The central panel records below the arms of a cross, the names of those killed. It is the same list as on the window memorial, but this time with the addition of an eighth name - Private George Jones of "B" Company, 2nd Border Regiment. The son of Edward and Elizabeth Jones (of Grange Cottage, Kingstone) twenty-one year old George had worked for a Kilpeck farmer before joining the Herefordshire Regiment in March, 1916. He was invalided home (records Bob and Jenny Davies) with trench foot during the following winter.

Returning to France in July, 1917, George was this time posted to the 2nd Border Regiment. The battalion at that time (having suffered heavy losses at Arras in the previous May) resting and refitting in the Mory area. Here drafts of no fewer than three hundred and ninety men joined during August. Moving to Saulty at the end of the month, the battalion there entrained for Proven. On to Oudezeele (1 September) and by the beginning of October the battalion was in camp close to Dickebush.

Now in the Ypres Salient, the men on 2 October were marched to dug-outs on the west side of Zillebeke Lake where they would make preparations for a forthcoming attack. At 6 am on 4 October, 2nd Border went forward over ground described in the battalion records as, little better than a bog. But objectives were taken, and by 9.40 the men were hard-at-work strengthening and consolidating their gains. At daybreak on 5 October (the date of George Jones's death) the enemy's guns, however, had found their range and the battalion's line came under heavy bombardment. At the same time, notes the records, "....his snipers became very active." With no known grave, George Jones's name was placed on the Tyne Cot Memorial at Passchendaele.

ABENHALL - GLOUCESTERSHIRE

St. Michael's

The memorial at St. Michael's, Abenhall - a medieval church, but very little remaining of the original building - will be found just inside the entrance and on the south side of the nave. Mounted on wood, a brass plaque records the names of ten men from the village that fell in the Great War (those for 1939-1945 are on a plate below). See these again at Mitcheldean, just to the north-west across the A4136, where the Royal British Legion have erected a memorial cross in the churchyard at St. Michael and All Angels to the war dead from both areas.

ALLENSMORE - HEREFORDSHIRE

St. Andrew's

Dating from the late thirteenth century and taking its name from Alan de Plokenet, Allensmore lies off the A465 four miles south-west of Hereford. Its greatest notoriety occurring in May, 1605 when villagers initiated a six-week uprising ("The Herefordshire Commotion") after an excommunicate from the Church of England (Alice Wellington) was refused burial in St. Andrew's churchyard.

Enter St. Andrew's (rebuilt 1857, restored 1880) by its late-Norman south doorway, and there on the north wall of the nave can be seen the marble plaque erected by the Rev. James Elliot Grasett (vicar 1868-1914) to commemorate the death in France of his second son.

Elliot Blair Grasett was born at Allensmore Vicarage on 12 October, 1888, and "gallant and fearless to the last" (recalled his Commanding Officer) "he died as he would have wished himself, in front of his men." From St. Michael's College (Tenbury) and the Hereford Cathedral School, Elliot later went on to Jesus College, Cambridge from where he graduated in 1911. He would chose the Army as his career (gazetted second-lieutenant 16 August, 1911) and soon in India, became attached to the 1st South Lancashire Regiment - then stationed at Subathu. Having transferred to the Indian Army, Lieutenant Grasett would first serve in Egypt - where in early February, 1915 he was present during the repulse of the Turkish attack at the Suez Canal.

To France in the following August, and here, notes the *Official History of the Great War* (Military Operations France and Belgium 1915), "The 33rd and 69th

Punjabis had come from Egypt to replace exhausted units like the 6th Jats and 15th Sikhs [heavy casualties at Aubers Ridge and Festubert the previous May], for whom drafts of the right class were not available."

On 25 September (the "Battle of Loos") three subsidiary attacks were planed with the view of distracting the enemy's attention from the main battle area. Actions at Pietre, Bois Grenier and Bellewaarde being undertaken by units of the Indian Corps shortly before the main British assault near Loos itself. Delivered at 6 am, the "Action of Pietre" (official battle nomenclature) north of Neuve Chapelle was led by the 7th (Meerut) Division. Gas and un-cut wire hampered much of the advance - but on the left there would be more

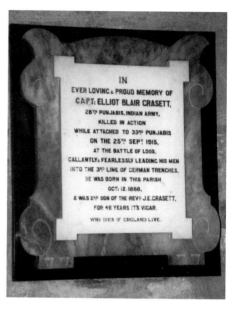

A gallant young officer killed at the head of his men. St. Andrew's, Allensmore.

success. All five battalions of the Bareilly Brigade storming the enemy's front trench with the bayonet and "....driving before them such Germans as appeared they reached the support trench. Here the Gurkhas halted, but the three leading battalions [1/4th Black Watch, 69th Punjabis, 2nd Black Watch] now reinforced by the 33rd Punjabis and 58th Rifles, continued the advance up the Moulin" [*Official History*]. By midday, however, the situation had became "alarming". The Bareilly Brigade (now with two long and open flanks, no reserves or support) being forced to retire with heavy losses after a strong and determined counter-attack by the enemy. The remnants of the brigade would be back in their original line by 4 pm. Captain Elliot Blair Grasett has no known grave and is commemorated on the Indian Memorial at Neuve Chapelle. Before leaving the church note its east window, this being dedicated to Elliot's mother.

Also on the north wall, the parish war memorial with the dedication "Sacred to the memory of the men of this parish who fell in the service of their country during the Great Wars." Below this there are eight names: Reuben Davies - Edward Gerrard - R. Thomas Gerrard - Eliot B. Grassett - Percy C. Galliers - John

Macklin - Robert Smith - and Ben Taylor for the First World War, and two for the Second. The latter being carved into the marble after 1945, together with the addition of the letter "S" to the last word of the dedication.

To the churchyard now, and here in the north section lies the Commonwealth War Graves Commission headstone of Private Robert C. Smith. Twenty-three when he died on 29 March, 1919, Robert Smith served with the 1st South Midland Mounted Brigade Field Ambulance, Royal Army Medical Corps - a Territorial Force unit with headquarters in Birmingham. His parents, Henry and Alice Smith, (records the CWGC) were resident at The Shop, Cobhall Common [west of] Allensmore.

East of the church we have a family plot, the headstone of which commemorates the deaths on the Western Front of two brothers. The sons of Richard and Mary Ann, Gunner Richard Thomas Gerrard of 177th Siege Battery, Royal Garrison Artillery, died (aged thirty-five) on 26 October, 1917, while his younger brother, Edward, was killed during operations on the Somme, 26 July, 1918. He served with the 38th Battalion, Machine Gun Corps and was twenty-two.

West of the church now and here commemorated is the eldest son of Albert Macklin. John Farr Macklin, who, having emigrated prior to the war, was killed in France on 11 March, 1918 while serving with the 57th Australian Infantry. His wife (Emily), records the CWGC, is noted as a resident of Wyalong, New South Wales.

ALVINGTON - GLOUCESTERSHIRE

St. Andrew's

The West Gloucestershire village of Alvington lies close to the River Severn on the A48 approximately six miles north-east of Chepstow - its church being of Early English and Decorated styles. On the north aisle of St. Andrew's, a white stone tablet has carved into its upper section, a cross. Either side are the dates 1914 and 1919, which are surrounded by roses and leaves, and below, a pattern of acorns and oak leaves provides a frame to the dedication and names of those that fell. The memorial records nine men, three of whom were brothers.

Private William James Andrews served with the 1st Monmouthshire Regiment. A battalion of the Territorial Force which had its Headquarters in Stow Hill, Newport. As Pioneer battalion to the 46th (North Midland) Division, the

Monmouths spent the summer of 1918 in the area around Bethune. The battalion had been in France since February, 1915 and in the lull that followed the German 1918 Spring offensive, was fully employed digging new, and maintaining existing, defensive positions.

As September opened, the enemy were again well established behind the heavily defended Hindenburg Line. Where, it was hoped, a strong defence could be maintained against the now advancing British forces. The Pioneers moved from Bethune to the neighbourhood of Beaucourt-sur-l'Hallue on 12 September and nine days later went forward from around Tetry to an old German trench system to the west of the St. Quentin Canal and facing the village of Bellenglise. Here the 1st Monmouths would have their work cut out maintaining the position, and putting it in a strong state of defence. The old trenches were very near to those of the Germans, so close, notes Major R.E. Priestley in his book *Breaking The Hindenburg Line,* that "Into Bellenglise itself, immediately below our trenches, it appeared possible to throw a cricket-ball, and every movement of the Germans in the neighbourhood of the Canal and the village was plainly to be seen." On 25 September, the 46th Division received its first orders regarding the forthcoming assault: "At an hour and date to be notified later, the 46th Division, as part of a major operation, will cross the St. Quentin Canal, Capture the Hindenburg Line, and advance...."

The main attack was planed for 29 September, but first a preliminary assault was to be made near Pontruet - an action in which Lieutenant J.C. Barrett of the 1/5th Leicestershire Regiment would be awarded the Victoria Cross. Here on 25 September, captured posts to the north and west of the village were consolidated by the Pioneers under heavy shell fire. On the next day, that which William Andrews was killed, the Monmouths were occupied on road-building and repairs. Private William James Andrews is buried in Brie British Cemetery, France.

Buried in the churchyard in a family grave south of the church is Private George James Evans of the Army Service Corps. The headstone gives his age, forty-six, and date of death as 27 July, 1919.

At 7.30 am on the opening day of the battle of the Somme - 1st July, 1916 - the 8th Gloucestershire Regiment moved forward to positions north of the town of Albert. Later, and by 10 pm, this battalion of Kitchener's "New Army" was located in the Tara-Usna Line, up in the forward area. On 3 July, the Gloucesters took part in the attack on La Boisselle. An action that would see their Commanding Officer, Lieutenant-Colonel A. Carton de Wiart, awarded the Victoria Cross. He was wounded during the battalion's next attack - the 23 July assault on the Switch Line.

The war diary of the 8th Gloucesters records that on 30 July, the date on which Henry Jones was killed, the battalion attacked the German Intermediate Line at 6.10 am. The advance being held up by enfilade machine gun fire and concealed snipers from the right. The men returned to their original line by 9.30 pm, where a roll call would establish that their had been casualties numbering one hundred and sixty-nine. Born in Aylburton, thirty-two year old Henry Jones lived with his wife Rosanna just a mile away at Alvington. He has no known grave and was commemorated on the Thiepval Memorial to the missing of the Somme.

Private Thomas Evan Joseph of the 1st Australian Infantry, and the first of the Joseph brothers to be killed, was thirty-one when he died on 3 October, 1917. Formed in New South Wales, the 1st Australians fought in Gallipoli (May-December, 1915) then on the Somme during the following year. On the Ypres Salient in 1917, the battalion took part in the Battle of the Menin Road (20-25 September) then from the 26th, the fighting at Polygon Wood. Thomas Joseph has no known grave and is commemorated on the Menin Gate Memorial to the missing.

It was during the fighting at Rosières on 27 March, 1918 that Sergeant Evan Victor Joseph won his Distinguished Conduct Medal. Having been driven back to the village the day before, the 1st Worcestershire Regiment took up defensive positions running from the eastern outskirts of Meharicourt. Here the order was given to hold this line at all costs: "....every man who is able to retire," instructed the Corps Commander, "is equally able to use his rifle or bayonet and will therefore maintain his place in the line until relieved."

In his history of the Worcestershire Regiment, Captain H. FitzM. Stacke, MC, records how dawn 27 March saw dense waves of the enemy pouring forward over the open slope beyond Meharicourt "All along the line guns and rifles opened fire, and under the rain of shells and bullets the first and second waves of the enemy dwindled and came to a halt...."

A fresh attack, however, reached the Worcester's trenches, but rapid fire from the defenders one again put the enemy to flight - leaving the road "strewn thick with their dead." Throughout the day's fighting, runs his DCM citation, Sergeant Joseph, who was responsible for the battalion's signallers "Under intense fire of shells and bullets repeatedly worked along the telephone lines repairing breaks and maintaining communication throughout the battle."

Sergeant Joseph is next mentioned in the records of the 1st Worcestershire on 13 October, 1918. His party of signallers working knee-deep in mud and water to set up a telephone line during the advance on Douai. Next day, while shells were exploding all around, he would add the Military Medal to his awards when seeing Captain E.G. Coxwell struck down by a shell, he went to his assistance - carrying the officer to safety. Wounded, Evan Joseph returned home where he subsequently died on 6 February, 1919. Aged thirty-two, Evan Joseph was married to Florence Joseph of 184 Coronation Road, Southville, Bristol, and buried at Arnos Vale Cemetery (see Thomas Stinchcombe below).

The third of the Joseph brothers to be killed, Maurice Llewellyn Joseph, served with the Army Service Corps before being transferred to the 2nd Royal Irish Rifles. On St. Patrick's Day, 17 March, 1918, the battalion were in reserve at Séraucourt, where, as part of the 36th

A father mourns three sons at St. Andrew's, Alvington.

(Ulster) Division, it was preparing for a strong German offensive around St. Quentin. This was to come four days later - the enemy at 4.30 am opening the day with a tremendous bombardment all along the British line. The most terrific, noted one observer, any man had ever seen.

By 4 pm, the 2nd RIR, still in reserve, would have suffered high casualties from the shelling. Then at 7 pm, one company of the battalion was ordered to attack - but its attempts to take back from the Germans the village of Contescourt met with even greater loss. Ordered to retire, the survivors fell back along the road where it was left to the Rifles to carry out a rearguard action. Covering, among other troops of the 36th Division, its own 1st Battalion. Gallantly performed, it would not be until 11 am, 22 March that the survivors were able to withdraw. This being the date of Maurice Joseph's death who, with no known grave, is commemorated on the Pozieres Memorial to the missing.

War Office records (*Soldiers Died In The Great War*) note that Rifleman Albert Parsloe was born in Alvington, enlisted into the Army at Lydney and initially served in the 11th Gloucestershire Regiment. This, a Reserve battalion of

Kitchener's "New Army", was, in September, 1916, redesignated as 16th Training Reserve Battalion. In 4th Reserve Brigade, this was located at Seaford. Sometime after this, Albert Parsloe would have been sent overseas, where in France, he was posted to the 16th King's Royal Rifle Corps. His date of death - he died from wounds received in action - was 23 April, 1917.

The 16th KRRC - formed September, 1914 from past and present members of the Church Lads Brigade - early in April, 1917 left Corbie on the Somme for the forward area. Souastre was reached on 8 April, Mercatel on the 12th, and Moyenneville, where the battalion was placed into reserve, 15 April. Here, records one member of the 16th, "The village was nothing but a ruin, but we made ourselves huts and shelters with the ample material to hand and were soon quite comfortable."

Operations against the German Hindenburg Line began 22 April and on this day the 16th KRRC went into action north of Croiselles. A failed assault which resulted in two hundred and sixty-nine casualties killed, wounded and missing. With no known grave - he was one of those posted as "missing" - Albert Parsloe's name is commemorated on the Arras Memorial at Faubourg-D'Amiens Cemetery.

The memorial gives William Henry Probert's regiment as 2nd Gloucestershire, but his headstone (opposite the tower on the west side of the church) bears the badge of the Cheshire Regiment. The Commonwealth War Graves Commission records note that he served as a private with the 7th Battalion and, as the son of H.C. Probert of Alvington Common, died on 17 October, 1917. His headstone also includes the words "Buried In This Churchyard," which indicates that his original grave has been lost.

In their cemeteries register for Gloucestershire, the Commonwealth War Graves Commission note that Arnos Vale Cemetery, Bristol contains three hundred and forty-nine British war graves. Some two hundred and forty of which are in a section designated as "Soldiers' Corner". A plot belonging to the Bristol branch of the British Red Cross Society, the graves are in the main those of soldiers who died in War Hospitals at Bristol - the 2nd Southern General and Beaufort in particular. Buried there is Private Thomas H. Curd Stinchcombe who served with the 1/5th Gloucestershire Regiment and died of cerebro spinal meningitis on 17 December, 1916. Aged thirty-three, he was married to Emily Elizabeth Stinchcombe of New House, Woolaston Common, Lydney.

Below the memorial, a small frame contains a Victory Medal, and two gold medals. Presented by the village to commemorate their service, one bears the name of Evan Joseph, the other that of his brother, Thomas. The reverse of each medal shows St. Andrew's church. Below the frame, another displays the hand-written words: "The Joseph Brothers were sons of the coachman of Clanna House. They fought in the Great War and were all killed. Their father died of a broken heart." Clanna (demolished after the Second World War, but a few farm buildings and cottages remain) - just across the A48 and to the north-west of Alvington - was the property of Captain W.B. Marling, JP.

The Commonwealth War Graves Commission record three war graves at St. Andrew's churchyard. Two of those buried, George Evans and William Probert, appear on the memorial within the church (see above), but a third is not shown. Opposite the tower on the west side of the church is the grave of Private George Gerald Merrick who was twenty-four when he died on 28 October, 1920. Having previously served with both the Somerset Light Infantry and Worcestershire Regiment (CWGC records) he was eventually wounded at Gaza while in the ranks of the 10th (Royal East Kent and West Kent Yeomanry) Battalion of the Buffs (East Kent Regiment). With the 74th (Yeomanry) Division, the 10th Buffs fought at both the Second and Third Battles of Gaza in 1917.

AVONMOUTH

St. Andrew's

Its foundation stone laid on 2 November, 1892, St. Andrew's in Richmond Terrace was constructed from local red (exterior) and Bath stone (interior) and consecrated on 27 July, 1893. Tragedy struck, however, when on 17 January, 1941 incendiary bombs fell onto the wooden roof - the subsequent fire causing great damage and the loss of many church possessions.

On the south wall at the front of the nave is the hoped-for reference to the Port of Avonmouth's work during the Great War. Presented by the St. Andrew's Soldiers' Home, a fine bronze plaque shows two roundels - one depicting a ship at sea, the other an artillery piece and tank. It was from Avonmouth, records *Bristol In The Great War,* by George F. Stone and Charles Wells, that tanks were first transported overseas. In raised letters, the dedication reads: "To the glory of God and the immortal memory of the men who passed through this port during the Great War 1914-1918, and met and defeated the enemy on sea and land and in the air, and by their sacrifice preserved our freedom and upheld the cause of justice and true Christian chivalry." Then a quotation: "Ye That Live On 'mid England's Pastures Green Remember Them, And Think What Might Have Been".

There are other First World War commemorations at St, Andrew's. Close to the entrance, a small brass plaque notes that the electric lighting was installed in October, 1921 when the original oak tablet, remembering those from the parish that were killed, was placed in the church. This being lost as a result of the 1941 fire damage.

To the left of the chancel is the church's Remembrance Corner. Dedicated by the Archdeacon of Bristol on Remembrance Sunday, 1991, it includes a Book of Remembrance and a three-section brass memorial that was brought to St. Andrew's from the now demolished Avonmouth Congregational Church - "The organ there having been installed to commemorate the coming of peace and perpetuate the men of Avonmouth (forty-four names recorded) that fell."

Their's lost in a fire, St. Andrew's, Avonmouth gives a new home to the memorial of a demolished church.

BACTON - HEREFORDSHIRE

St. Faith's

Dedicated to St. Faith (a third century martyr who was condemned to suffer on a gridiron before being beheaded) the church at Bacton dates from the early twelve hundreds. Bacton being situated in the Golden Valley, ten miles south-west of Hereford and on a minor road off the B4347.

Entering the church, the eye is immediately drawn to the north wall and the window dedicated to Reginald Gardener Partridge. Younger brother of Richard Crawshay Bailey Partridge and killed in South Africa during the Boer War. Both men volunteering for overseas service and leaving England on 2 February, 1900, Richard would be present when his brother was killed during a skirmish on the following 29 September.

Either side of the window, badges of the Shropshire Yeomanry are displayed on small wooden shields. To the right, one also includes Reginald's Queen's South Africa Medal ribbon, while on the left – those belonging to the Military Cross, QSA and French *Croix de Guerre* of his brother Richard are seen.

Chairman of the family company since the death of his father in 1909, Richard Partridge would also lose his life, ironically eighteen years, almost to the day, after that of his brother and exactly four years from the date (28 September, 1914) of his first Commission.

It would appear that Richard Partridge did not sail with the 1/1st Shropshire Yeomanry when it left for Egypt on 4 March, 1916. The *Monthly Army List* for this time showing him as being posted to the 2nd Regiment which remained at home. By March, 1917, however, he is given as attached to the 7th King's Shropshire Light Infantry and at some time joined that battalion in France.

Parish memorial, St. Faith's, Bacton.

The *London Gazette* dated 16 September, 1918 notes the award of his Military Cross: "For conspicuous gallantry and devotion to duty during operations lasting eleven days, especially on one occasion when heavy shelling was on. This officer first got away the horses of the M.M.P. [Military Mounted Police], and then went to the wagon lines of a R.F.A. [Royal Field Artillery] brigade, where many casualties were occurring, and collected a party to remove the horses. His prompt action no doubt saved a number of casualties."

The French *Croix de Guerre* was also awarded. This being notified in the *London Gazette* for 8 October, just after his death near Havrincourt Wood on 28 September, 1918. Also situated at the window is a framed photograph of Richard Partridge, and close by a fine marble tablet giving date and details of his death. Once again, the Shropshire Yeomanry badge, and medal ribbons are shown in full colour. Captain Partridge is buried at Beaumetz Cross Roads Cemetery, France and is also commemorated at St. Mary's Church, Abbeydore, close to Bacton.

Turning now to face south, colour is again dominant in a white marble tablet. This time featuring the figure of St. George who looks across to finely carved letters commemorating the death of Arthur John Wheeler at Gallipoli.

Arthur John Wheeler memorial, St. Faith's, Bacton.

Having landed at "S" Beach, Helles the previous April, 2nd South Wales Borderers during the early hours of 6 July were making preparations for an attack on Turkish positions at Gully Ravine. Just across from their positions in trenches - "J11" and "J11b" - the enemy were busy constructing a knoll that later became known as the "Gridiron".

Ten men under Lieutenant P.H. Turner were first in action. Going forward at 2.30 am - rushing the Turkish garrison and killing many. Close behind, another party soon began work constructing a sandbag wall. But having been alerted, the Turks quickly opened fire with three machine guns - this being followed up by a strong counter-attack, which, out-manned and out-bombed, soon forced the Borderers to retire. Total casualties: two officers and thirteen other ranks killed, thirty wounded.

Both Richard Partridge and Arthur Wheeler appear on the parish memorial situated on the north wall at St. Faiths. Once again, a fine white marble tablet illuminated with red, blue and gold. There are six names in total, the first of the remaining four being Alfred Smith.

The 7th King's Shropshire Light Infantry had arrived in the Somme area on 1 July, 1916. The first day of the great battle. From Fienvillers the battalion reached the ruins of Carnoy on 7 July, and two weeks later took part in its first major action - some four hundred casualties being suffered during an attack on the enemy's support line running between the villages of Longueval and Bazentine-le-Grande. "Lonely Trench", later renamed "Shropshire", was taken on 19 August.

On 13 November, 1916 (the date of twenty-one-year-old Alfred Smith's death) 7th KSLI were given the task of assaulting Serre - one of a series of heavily fortified villages situated close to the River Ancre. At 5.45 am ("Zero Hour") the men went forward through thick-fog and pitch-darkness. Deep mud, in many places up to the mens' waists, would also hold up progress.

Richard Crawshay Bailey memorial, St. Faith's, Bacton.

Although classed as a failure, the 13 November attack on Serre saw part of the German front line taken and occupied. But only a small part could be held. Those desperately attempting to bring food, ammunition and stores forward, taking four hours to cover a one-thousand-yard journey. When relieved on 14 November, 7 KSLI had suffered over two hundred and twenty casualties - killed, wounded and missing. Private Alfred Smith is buried in Serre Road Cemetery No.1.

Thirty-one, and the husband of Bertha Hill, Private Alexander Thomas Henry Hill was wounded on 20 September, 1917 and subsequently died at Newcastle Military Hospital on 20 November. Two months previous (on 19 September) the 6th King's Shropshire Light Infantry formed up at Alouette Farm, close to the village of Langemarck on the Ypres Salient. Here they were waiting in readiness for an attack next day. Having gone into action at 5.40 am, "D" Company would soon reach the enemy's line known as "White Trench" - but here they would come under intense machine gun fire. Casualties were also suffered by "A" Company - as they advanced along with both "B" and "C" - who were heavily shelled. A later assault on "Eagle Trench" (notes regimental historian Major W. de B. Wood) was held up by a "tornado of bombs." Alexander Hill's body was brought home to Bacton and buried close to the church on its east side. The inscription on the headstone including much information.

Arthur George Spreadborough was killed while his battalion, the 7th King's Shropshire Light Infantry, held shallow trenches close to the Hindenburg Line and in front of Héninel. The men having fell back to these positions during the night of 22 March, 1918 after a heavy German offensive. On the morning of 24 March an attempt by the enemy to rush the KSLI trenches was successfully repulsed. In the same way another effort made during the afternoon saw the attackers driven off. The next two days, notes the battalion records, were spent in re-adjusting the Divisional front - the 7th KSLI during that period holding the front line west of Hénlin-sur-Cojenl.

Farrier-Sergeant George Pritchard served with "G" Battery, 5th Army Brigade, Royal Horse Artillery and was twenty-six when he died from bronchial pneumonia at Etaples Military Hospital on 23 October, 1918. As part of Fourth Army, the 5th Army Brigade, RHA, during the months leading up to George Pritchard's death, had seen action on the Somme (in August) and taken part in the September/October battles of the Hindenburg Line.

BELMONT - HEREFORDSHIRE

St. Michael's Abbey

Just a short distance south-west of Hereford (off the A465) St. Michael's Abbey - a stone building in Decorated Gothic style - was completed in 1856 and built on the Belmont estate through the generosity of local landowner Mr. Francis Richard Wegg-Prosser. The Wegg-Prosser family lived close-by at Belmont House (now a golf club) and provided the abbey for use by the Benedictines then at Newport. Began in 1857, the monastery was officially opened on 21 November, 1859.

The Wegg-Prossers occupy a burial ground to the side of the abbey and it is in this area that we find a Calvary looking down on their graves. This bearing a plaque mentioning the death in 1916 of Second-Lieutenant Cecil Francis Wegg-Prosser - grandson of Francis Richard. The only child of Major Francis Wegg-Prosser, Cecil was born in 1892 and having been educated at Beaumont College, Old Windsor, and Trinity, Cambridge, he took his BA Degree in June, 1914. Reading for the Bar when war was declared, he at once volunteered for military duty. Serving first with the Inns of Court OTC, then (in April, 1915) receiving a Commission in the Royal Sussex Regiment. Posted in January, 1916, he went to his father's regiment (the Rifle Brigade) and having been ordered overseas in the following July, joined its 16th Battalion in France.

On the Somme, and north of the River Ancre, the 16th Rifle Brigade were (on 3 September, 1916) to help secure a few hundred yards of high ground, west-north-west of the village of St. Piere-Divion. This to cover the flank of the 49th Division advancing up the valley. Attacking on the left, the 16th fought desperately to gain their objectives – but all failed. The battalion losing more than four hundred and fifty killed, wounded or missing – one of those to fall being Cecil Wegg-Prosser. Of his death, his Commanding Officer wrote: "He was the first man of this Battalion into the German trenches and was instantaneously killed, being shot through the heart as he topped the German parapet. Few alas! of his men came back, but the few who did speak with one voice of his great gallantry." With no known grave, Cecil Francis Prosser is commemorated on the Thiepval Memorial to the missing of the Somme.

Second-Lieutenant Cecil Francis Wegg-Prosser remembered at Belmont Abbey.

Also in the burial ground is the grave of Fleet Surgeon J. Moore of HMS *Pembroke* who died 13 May, 1915. Then, close to the path on the south side, a wife remembers her husband on the headstone of her grave. Second-Lieutenant Wilfred John Massey-Lynch being killed in France on 4 April, 1918 while serving with the 3rd Dragoon Guards. On this day the regiment had been ordered forward to positions north-east of Villers Bretonneux where the enemy, having forced the British 14th Division out of their trenches around the Bois de Vaire, were massing for another attack. Moving up under heavy fire and in drenching rain the men dismounted and forming a defensive flank south of the Fouilloy-Warfusée road, immediately came into action. The situation was, records the Regimental records, in hand by noon – the rest of the day passing "fairly quietly".

Twenty-five-year-old Wilfred Massey-Lynch has no known grave and is commemorated on the Pozieres Memorial on the Somme. The Commonwealth War Graves Commission register (published 1928) for which records that Wilfred's parents (Thomas and Lisle) were resident at Forge Lodge, Blundellsands, Liverpool, and that his wife (Gwen) lived at Lyncheston, Belmont.

BLAKENEY – GLOUCESTERSHIRE

All Saints

"Be thou faithful unto death, and I will give thee a crown of life". These words from *Revelation* (ch. 21, v. 10) illustrated in a fine window on the north side of All Saints. A stone church built c1820 by Samuel Hewlett (restored 1907) and comprising nave, small chancel, south porch and narrow western tower – Blakeney lying between the Forest of Dean and the River Severn, south-west of Gloucestershire on the A48. As the parish war memorial, the window is accompanied by a slab of white marble. Expertly carved in the form of a scroll and recording the names, ranks and regiments of those that were killed.

A fine window and marble scroll at All Saints, Blakeney.

Not mentioned on the memorial is Private Frederick Jones (Royal Army Medical Corps) who having died 2 October, 1918, was buried in the churchyard. This located approximately one hundred and fifty yards west of the church. Two names – James Willetts (aged twenty-three and killed in action 15 March, 1917) and Francis Hale (twenty-two, 20 August, 1916) – are also commemorated on family headstones in another churchyard. That of Blakeney Independent Chapel situated on the main road below All Saints.

BRIDSTOW – HEREFORDSHIRE

Close to the River Wye, Bridstow lies near to Ross (just over a mile to the east) or Hereford some twelve miles further to the north-west. Turning off the A40, then west onto the A49, the parish memorial (a stone cross mounted on a four-sided base) appears after a short distance on the right. Bridstow, which also took in the hamlet of Wilton, had a population of five hundred and seventy-eight in 1914 – some twenty of whom were not to return from the Great War and have their names recorded on the base of the cross.

St. Bridget's

A short drive now along the lane signposted "Golf Club" and we come to St. Bridget's. Consecrated here in 1066 and completely rebuilt – save for the late fourteenth-century west tower – by Thomas Nicholson in 1862. Walk through the south porch and ahead on the north side is the window dedicated to Captain John Ramsay Cox. An officer of the Worcestershire Regiment who – the son of Church Warden Captain William Stanley Ramsay Cox – was killed at Neuve Chapelle on 12 March, 1915.

Twenty men remembered at Bridstow - six more added for the Second World War.

During the first days of March, 1915, records Captain H. FitzM. Stacke, MC in his history of the Worcestershire Regiment, the trenches held by the 1st Battalion in front of Neuve Chapelle were subject to much activity. Officers from a number of regiments being sent up in order to reconnoitre the ground in preparation for the great attack planned to commence on the 10th. This to smash through the salient in the German line formed by the village of Neuve Chapelle, then hopefully on to take the Aubers Ridge.

Parties of the 1st Worcestershire were in action shortly after the barrage (the heaviest bombardment yet experienced in the war) lifted to the rear of the village around 8 am. In reserve, however, the main body of the battalion would moved forward later and during the afternoon, two companies were heavily engaged. But the following day would be full of disaster – heavy casualties as the Worcesters advanced (the number being increased due to our own shells falling short); a shortage of ammunition and orders.

Before first daylight on 12 March, the enemy's guns heavily shelled the Worcestershire trenches. Then through the mist a dense mass of enemy infantry were seen surging forward. Two battalions of the 21st Bavarian Reserve Regiment in close formation lead by officers waving swords, noted one eyewitness, and followed by "a fat old blighter on a horse."

St. Bridget's, Bridstow. The church remembers its dead on a memorial to the left, and the son of one of its churchwardens to the right.

"On the right of the Worcestershire the Sherwoods suddenly fell back. The little salient which their line formed had been attacked from both sides and broken in." This was to leave the Worcester's right flank open "....but the Battalion remained unshaken. 'A' Company swiftly formed to the right to face the opened flank and the abandoned trenches of the Foresters." One officer of "A" Company noted "A most extraordinary hush for a few seconds as we held our fire while they closed in on us." The Bavarians now within seventy yards – "From flank to flank the whole line of the Worcestershire broke into the crackling roar of rapid fire. We brought them down in solid chunks. Down went the officers, the sergeant majors and the old blighter on the horse."

At this point the Worcester's broke from their line and charged into the Bavarians. Bayoneting and firing as they went. Much of the enemy now scattered and found its way into an orchard where, reported *The Times* for 19 April, 1915 – "The Worcesters had a fine scrap with the Germans. The Worcesters had their tails up with a vengeance. They chased the Germans up and down that muddy field like terriers after a rats."

Meanwhile to the left of "A" Company, "B", "C" and "D" were also engaged in a fierce bayonet fight. The end of which saw "....the pursued beaten enemy into their own lines." Storming a group of building known as "Point 85", the Worcestershire occupied these. But once again, through lack of communication, the British guns inflicted casualties among its own troops via sporadic bombardment of the captured area.

Now isolated, the three companies beat off counter-attack after counter-attack until at about 10 am, when it had became clear that the battalion's position (now encircled by the enemy on three sides, and, notes Captain Stacke, "....shelled by both artilleries....") was no longer tenable. Reluctantly the Commanding Officer, Colonel E.C.F. Wodehouse gave the order to fall back.

As the three companies withdrew in good order "....officers and men fell fast. The Commanding Officer, the Adjutant, and the last surviving Company Commanders went down, and it was a mere remnant of the three stubborn companies which, still in good order and grimly firing, reached the trenches which they had held at dawn."

Still away to the right, the survivors of "A" Company, now with hardly any officers, continued the fight in the orchard. But here too, lack of support inevitably forced a withdrawal. The four companies now reunited, the Roll was taken and casualties counted. The day's fighting had amounted to a total of three hundred and seventy all ranks. With no known grave, John Cox's name appears on the Le Touret Memorial to the missing

John Cox was born 29 June, 1873 and educated at Bruton School, Somerset. He had prior to the First World War served with the 6th (Special Reserve) Battalion, Worcestershire Regiment, rejoining early in September, 1914. Having been attached to the 11th Worcestershire, and temporally employed as a Staff Captain at 78th Infantry Brigade Headquarters, he proceeded to France in early January, 1915 as part of a draft for the 1st Worcestershire.

Moving now to the south aisle, here to the right of the Norman arch that leads to the chancel, we find another parish memorial. This time in the form of a tablet erected by the parishioners in March, 1922. Here the same twenty names are listed, but now with the addition of ranks and regiment.

Still on the south side of the church we find another plaque connected with the Great War. Brass this time and bearing the regimental badge and motto - *Quis Separabit* (Who shall separate us) - of the Royal Irish Rifles. Below the badge an inscription that tells much about an old and gallant soldier: "In loving memory of Herbert Clifford Bernard, Colonel Indian Army, sometime in command of Rattray's Sikhs, who was killed at Thiepval 1 July 1916, while gallantly leading his regiment, 10th Royal Irish Rifles."

Born in Cheltenham (his father at one-time Deputy Inspector General of Hospitals and Fleets) Colonel Bernard had fought in the Burmese War of 1885-

1891 and was Commandant of the 45th (Rattray's) Sikhs Regiment from 1909 until his retirement early in 1914. Quickly formed when war was declared in August, 1914 was Kitchener's "New Army". Made up entirely of volunteers, it would be the experienced, old and often retired soldiers of all ranks that would take responsibility of command and training. So it was that Colonel Bernard took command of one such formation - the 10th (Service) Battalion, Royal Irish Rifles (South Belfast) Part of the 36th (Ulster) Division.

Having landing in France with his battalion, the Colonel, now in his fiftieth year would lead his men forward from Aveluy Wood, across the River Ancre, and into the western edge of Thiepval Wood. It was the early hours of 1 July, 1916 and the first day of the great "Battle of the Somme" was about to begin. In reserve for the time being, the Rifles would have an hour to wait before going forward. An hour in which they would see other men of the 36th (Ulster) Division leave their trenches and in good and steady order enter no-man's-land. The men of the 10th Rifles would also witness the devastation that followed - machine gun bullets and shell cutting through the ranks of the Ulstermen as they disappeared into the smoke. But the Rifles would themselves come under fire - Colonel Bernard being one of the first to be hit as he stood at the head of his men. His body was taken back and later buried in Martinsart British Cemetery on the south side of the village and the road to Aveluy.

To the churchyard now and the section that lies to the south-east of the church. Look for a dark stone cross, this marking a Sainsbury family grave, and from this we learn how on 31 January, 1919, Partridge George Sainsbury died "Due to the effects of war." Thirty-five-years-old, he had served as a sergeant with the Worcestershire Yeomanry, but did not, according to regimental records, go overseas. Both he and his father are listed in the 1913 edition of *Kelly's Directory of Herefordshire and Shropshire,* as Farmers and Dairymen of Whitecross and Church Farms.

Before leaving St. Bridget's walk across the road to the churchyard extension where upon entering the gate, the eye is immediately drawn to a regimental badge carved into a tall headstone. Below this the inscription tells how, erected by the Commissioners of the Royal Hospital Chelsea, the stone marks the final resting place of five old soldiers. Soldiers who, according to their dates of death during the 1940s, were possible veterans of 1914-1918 and resident in the area as in-pensioners at the nearby Moraston House.

Look to the left now and moving along we come to the first of two graves whose headstones also commemorate family members that died while serving in the Great War. A Celtic cross belonging to the Gwyne family tells how a son, twenty-year-old Albert Edward Gwyne, was killed in action on 19 August, 1917 while in France. He was from Weirend, just to the south-west of Bridstow, and was with the 14th Gloucestershire Regiment at Lempire when he died. The battalion war diary for that day recording how, after an attack by 105th Brigade, the 14th Gloucestershire were engaged throughout the night wiring the newly gained trenches. Casualties are noted as one killed and four wounded.

Little information can be gleaned regarding the soldier commemorated on his wife's Gothic-style headstone further along to the left. No records so-far having been found regarding the Sergeant T.R. Bennetts (14th Canadian Battalion) mentioned.

BRISTOL

Cathedral

Entering Bristol Cathedral - it was founded in 1140 - first walk along the north aisle where up above can be seen A.W. Robinson's fine collection of windows depicting Bristol's auxiliary forces of the Second World War. But below these we see our first reference to the First World War - a small brass plaque informing that "The above Union Jack and Red Cross were flown over Headquarters 2nd Southern General Hospital (Territorial) Bristol, through which over 89,000 sick & wounded passed during the Great War 1914-1919." The HQ referred to was at Colston Fort, Montague Place, Kingsdown.

Another Royal Army Medical Corps unit based at Bristol (also Kingsdown) was the 3rd South Midland Field Ambulance and like

Stretcher bearers, orderlies and drivers - RAMC men from Bristol - their badges once proudly worn and now on their memorial at Bristol Cathedral.

other Territorial Force formations at the outbreak of war created duplicate units. In this way the original would change its numerical designation to 1/3rd, the duplicate then taking the title of 2/3rd.

Across to the south aisle now and here on another small brass tablet a similar reference to that we have just left: "The above Union Jack and Red Cross were flown over the dressing station of the 1/3rd S. Midland Field Ambulance on the Asiago Plateau, Italy July to October 1918." As part of the 48th (South Midland) Division, 1/3rd South Midland Field Ambulance had first served in France and Flanders (Battles of the Somme and Ypres) before moving to Italy at the end of November, 1917. Beneath this a larger brass tablet records below the badge of the Royal Army Medical Corps the names of the twenty-one men that lost their lives during the unit's war service.

Remembering eight choristers at Bristol Cathedral. Their voices heard no more.

Surmounting a finely sculptured bronze memorial to those of the 2/3rd South Midland Field Ambulance that were killed (sixteen names), the RAMC badge is again featured. The 61st Division this time which, having crossed to France in May, 1916, would be in time for the 19 July action at Fromelles – before serving through Ypres, Cambrai, and the Somme. Note just above the names, the inclusion of the 61st Divisional sign. An ingenious device made up of the Roman numeral LXI.

Still on the south side of the cathedral we make our way now to the sign directing us to the chapter house – but before doing this look for a G.J. Hunt window – this in commemoration of the officers and men of the Royal Naval Volunteer Reserve (Bristol Division) and those recruited in Bristol and the West that served in the Royal Naval Division during the First World War. Enter the doorway leading to the chapter house and there on the stairway a fine mosaic erected 15 May, 1920 by the Cathedral Old Choristers Association commemorates eight of their number that were killed.

Saint Mary on the Quay

Built by R.S. Pope in 1840, St. Mary's with its grand portico of six fluted Corinthian columns, looks down onto the city centre - the river that once flowed past its door unseen since the area was built over in 1891/93. On the wall outside the church a brass tablet tells how five hundred and forty-five men of St. Mary's School and congregation, joined up in the Great War - sixty-seven of which lost their lives.

In raised letters, the names of the dead are recorded in four columns - and there heading the list we see one George Archer-Shee. Nineteen when he died on 31 October, 1914, having been mortally wounded the day before as his battalion, the 1st South Staffordshire Regiments, defended positions around Gheluvelt on the Menin road east of Ypres.

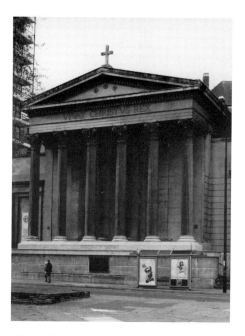

Corinthian columns stand guard over the names of sixty-seven church members that were killed. St. Mary on the Quay, Bristol.

But it is the years just prior to the war that are of interest here. As a thirteen-year-old naval cadet at Osbourne College, former St. Mary's altar boy, George Archer-Shee was accused of stealing a five-shilling postal order and subsequently expelled. But convinced of his innocence his family fought to clear the boy's name. A case against the Admiralty that caused great interest throughout the country - Edward Carson (well known for his work in the Oscar Wilde/Marquis of Queensbury liable case) serving as the family's barrister - and subsequently saw the awarded in damages to the Archer-Shee's of £3,000. A familiar story? Well yes. George Archer-Shee was the real Ronnie Winslow - main character in Terrance Rattigan's play (later film) based on the case - *The Winslow Boy.*

Wills Memorial Building (University of Bristol)

Dominating the skyline as you look up Park Street from the city centre, the University's main building was opened by His Majesty King George V on 9 June,

1925. Designed by Sir George Oatley in the Gothic Perpendicular style, this prominent Bristol landmark was the gift of Sir George A. Wills and Mr. Henry Herbert Wills as a memorial to their father, Henry Overton Wills. Founder and first Chancellor of the University.

From the entrance hall climb the massive double staircase to the first floor and there on the landing the University's Roll of Honour in the form of two marble tablets. Second World War to the right, First on the left, both have no dedication and record alphabetically the names in linear form. A total of one hundred and seventy-three for the 1914-1919 period.

CHRISTCHURCH - GLOUCESTERSHIRE

David Verey notes in Pevsner's *Buildings of England* (Gloucestershire: The Vale and the Forest of Dean edition) that the church at Christchurch was the first to be built in the nineteenth century (1812) within the Forest of Dean. Being of Gothic style and comprising nave, chancel, north aisle and embattled western tower. The parish itself, north of Coleford, was formed in 1844 and included Joyford, Hillersland, Shortstanding, Edge End and part of Berry Hill - all in the township of West Dean (Kelly's).

Enter the church, and immediately on the wall to the right of the door is a brass plaque - erected by the Christchurch and District Red Cross Committee, and made by F. Osborne & Co. Ltd of London - recording the names of twenty-four men that lost their lives in the First World War. Below the plaque is a small shelf on which is placed several brass flower-vases. Close inspection revealing that two of these carry engraved dedications commemorating two young men that fell within days of each other. From Coleford, twenty-one-year-old Bert Gwilliam, killed 4 October, 1917 and a year older, Frank Young, a Berry Hill boy who died 7 October. Both served with the 12th Gloucestershire Regiment - formed in Bristol during the early weeks of the war.

In *"Bristol's Own"* - the reminiscences of an original member of the 12th Gloucesters, and published in the *Western Daily Press* - the author notes how "The battalion went into action in these delectable surroundings [trenches on the Menin road, Inverness Copse sector] on Monday, October 1, and were right in the middle of the soup for ten whole days. Even on the way up, by way of Sanctuary Wood - another health resort - we had casualties." Turning now to the battalion war diary, and the days relevant to the men's deaths, we find that while moving forward in support of an attack at 6.40 am, 4 October, there would be some one hundred and fifty casualties. The enemy's guns being noted as "....very active during this operation." On 7 October the German guns are again referred to "....very quiet during the morning, but the duck-boards and trenches were shelled by the enemy during the evening...."

To the pulpit now and there above we see an oak hymn-board dedicated to Jocelyn Alfred Millard who "....lost his life on war service in H.M. Submarine *E4* on August 15th, 1916 aged 26 years." It was on 15 August, 1916 that the *E4* sank in collision with another submarine (the *E41)* off Harwich. Later raised, the bodies of those that died were taken ashore at Shotley, and subsequently buried in the Naval Reservation at St. Mary's churchyard.

A brass tablet and vases for two of "Bristol's Own" at Christchurch.

CLEHONGER - HEREFORDSHIRE

All Saints

Close to the Wye, Clehonger lies just south-west of Hereford - most of All Saints, notes the church guide, being built during the thirteenth century. Sadly, the inscription on the tall cross on the north side of the churchyard is worn, but as the parish war memorial the names of the twelve men who fell in the Great War can just be seen - "and when they had served their generation, they fell on sleep", notes the inscription.

Move now towards the porch on the south side, and close by will be found two Gothic-style headstones belonging to the Nash family. There too, in the same plot, another erected by the Commonwealth War Graves Commission and commemorating the death on 22 February, 1917 of Sapper T.G. Nash. From the headstone on the right, we learn that Trevor George Nash, an employee of the London and North Western Railway at their Abergavenny Manager's Office, having joined the Royal Engineers Railway Operating Division, died while at Frensham Hill Military Hospital in Farnham, Surrey in his twentieth year. He lies now beside Henry, his father, and his mother Juliette Emily.

Railwayman Trevor George Nash at rest in All Saints churchyard, Clehonger.

Note, just in front of the lychgate, the family cross that also commemorates the death in France on 21 August, 1917, of Harold Thomas Read. Born 9 November, 1889 and killed in action while serving with the 29th (Vancouver) Battalion, Canadian Expeditionary Force. Before leaving All Saints churchyard, see if you can spot, due south of the porch, a small cross with the word "Waterloo" on its base. This in memory of Private Benjamin Preece, 1st Dragoon Guards - a veteran of the great battle of 1815 who died, aged eighty-seven, in 1870.

A tall family cross near the lychgate of All Saints, Clehonger remembers Harold Thomas Read. Killed in action while serving with a Canadian regiment.

DOWN HATHERLEY - GLOUCESTERSHIRE

Church of St. Mary and Corpus Christi

Just north-north-east of Gloucester, off the Tewkesbury road (A38), Down Hatherley lies to the east. Its church of St. Mary and Corpus Christi being rebuilt in 1859 (save for its fifteenth-century perpendicular west tower) and comprising chancel, nave of four bays, and north aisle. It is in the north aisle that we see a pair of fine windows by A.L. Mootetson of London, dedicated to a young cavalry officer who was killed in action on 13 May, 1915 near Ypres.

Thomas Villiers Tuthill Thacker Neville

Thomas Villiers Tuthill Thacker Neville was born 12 August, 1880 at Borrismore (Co. Kilkenny), and educated at St. Columba's College and Trinity College, Dublin. He went into the Army in May, 1900 (gazetted second-lieutenant, 3rd Dragoon Guards) and later saw service in South Africa. With the rank of captain, he went with his regiment to France on 31 October, 1914 - sailing from Southampton on the SS *Victorian.*

Later in Belgium, the 3rd Dragoon Guards would see much fighting around Ypres - both in the first battle, and again in 1915. On 8 May, 1915 the Germans would make another determined effort to take Ypres itself by breaking through at Frezenberg. Next day, the 3rd Dragoon Guards came forward in motor-buses to Brielen - a small village about two miles north-west of Ypres - and three hundred strong (Thomas Neville would be among the officers) the regiment at 8 pm on 12 May moved up through Ypres then on to positions north of the Bellewarde Lake and close to the railway line running out of Potijze. Poor trenches that were in places no more than two feet deep. "'A' Squadron under Captain Neville, thickened its parapets, while the left troop made a barricade on the railway." (Holt).

"All was quiet on the Regiment's front until daybreak on the 13th...." (Holt) then the enemy's artillery opened up with, what was to go on record as the "heaviest bombardment experienced so far during the war." Then the infantry

Two fine windows by A.L. Mootetson to the memory of Thomas Neville at St. Mary and Corpus Christi, Down Hatherley.

came on with great determination "....especially against 'A' Squadron [heavily bombarded and attacked from both front and rear], but thanks to their good shooting, not a man got within 100 yards of the trench." Four other attacks during the day were similarly repulsed, but at 5pm Captain Neville was wounded. He died the same evening.

Close to the Neville windows, and to the left of the chancel arch, is a bronze plaque commemorating Anthoney Gilbert Jones, who died at Hatherley Court on 4 October, 1887, and his widow, Elizabeth, who passed away 21 February, 1909. But below their names there are details of two First World War officers - a great grandson, Captain Frederick Hatherley Bruce Selous, and Second-Lieutenant Jaffrey Fryer Selous Jones - a grandson.

From Worplesdon in Surrey, Frederick Selous went to Rugby in 1912 and it is with thanks to that school's records (*Memorials of Rugbeians who fell in the Great*

War Volume VI) that we know much about this young flying-officer. From Rugby in 1915, he entered the Royal Military College, Sandhurst - leaving in April, 1916, having been gazetted to the Queen's (Royal West Surrey Regiment). After training as a pilot with the Royal Flying Corps, he went to France in July, 1916 and during his nine months service there was awarded the Italian Silver Medal for Military Valour. Returning to England in April, 1917 (his award of the Military Cross "for distinguished service in the Field" coming through in the following June) Frederick Selous joined the Central Flying School as an instructor.

Returning to France in September, 1917, he would be killed whilst leading his Flight over the German lines near Roulers (on the Menin Road) 4 January, 1918.

Frederick Selous - a great grandson and pilot remembered at St. Mary and Corpus Christi, Down Hatherley. Killed a year to the day after his famous father.

A brother officer of No. 60 Squadron wrote the following account of his death: "I was up at 15,000 feet over the German lines on January 4th in company with my Squadron leader, Captain Selous. All at once both wings of his aeroplane suddenly collapsed and the machine fell like a stone to the earth. We are all terribly upset at this, as he was idolized by us all."

Nineteen-year-old Frederick's contribution would be added to that of his father. Captain Frederick Courteney Selous, DSO (professional big-game hunter and writer of many travel books on Africa) losing his life - ironically a year to the day (4 January, 1917) before that of his son - while serving in East Africa with the 25th Royal Fusiliers. He was sixty-five.

Twenty-four when he died was Royal Engineers officer Second-Lieutenant Jaffrey Fryer Selous Jones. Dying on 26 August, 1916 from wounds received at High Wood on the Somme, Jaffrey served with the "Special Brigade" - the secret unit raised by Sir John French in June, 1915 to carry out gas operations.

The Down Hatherley parish memorial is located on the north side of the church, close to the main entrance. A bronze plaque and commemorating four men: Thomas Wheeler, Albert John Priday, Henry George Smith, who was awarded the Military Medal, and John Davis.

Before leaving St. Mary's visit the grave of Driver Francis Roberts on the south side of the churchyard. From Fir Tree Cottage, Down Hatherley, he served with the Army Service Corps and died 11 January, 1921.

DRYBROOK - GLOUCESTERSHIRE

Holy Trinity

"Our Forest Church is a special place,/This tower topped building with a grey stone face./Set on a hillside - where all may see,/It is a spiritual home for folk like me." These four lines are taken from a poem printed in the church guidebook - which also tells how the foundation stone was laid at Holy Trinity on 4 June, 1816 and its first service held just eight months later on 2 February, 1817. In the Forest of Dean, Drybrook lies off the A4136 north of Cinderford.

Entering Holy Trinity, the eye is immediately drawn to the south side of the nave where, flanked by two Royal British Legion Standards, we see the parish war memorial in the centre of which a brass plaque tells how " To the glory of God and in loving memory of the following men who fell in the Great War, a peal of 8 bells was erected in this tower September 1919." The plaque, erected there by the "Drybrook and District Comrades of the Great War" goes on to list the names of forty-seven men that lost their lives - these listed in groups according to residence - The Morse (2), Harry Hill (5), Drybrook (6), The Hawthorn (1), Ruardean Hill (6), Wigpool (1), Plump Hill (3), Steam Mills (5), Ruardean Woodside (2), Nailbridge (1), Hawkwell (2), Brierley (1), Cinderford (4),

The tower at Holy Trinity, Drybrook looks down on one village memorial.

Upper Bilson (3), Bilson (5). Of those listed, no less than five have the surname of Meek.

Made from oak, the memorial, in addition to the brass tablet already mentioned, has a further six sections listing, again by residence, the names of those that served. Two hundred and forty-seven this time - Drybrook (44), Steam Mills (19), Morse Road (23), Ruardean Hill (38), Woodside (31), Brierley (16), Upper Bilson (38), Plump Hill (16), Harrow Hill (22). With a total of twenty-three, once again the name of Meek is prominent. Note also the two small brass flower-vases. These presented "in memory of the fallen" by their parents and friends.

Sapper A. Harris commemorated on a family headstone at Holy Trinity, Drybrook. His rifle drapes the cross.

Seven of those recorded on the brass plaque to those that died are buried within the churchyard - Private William Thomson George (Machine Gun Corps, died, aged twenty-five on 18 October, 1918), Private Hubert Hall (13th Gloucestershire Regiment, died 18 March, 1917 from wounds received in France. He was twenty-five), Sergeant Benjamin Hope, also 13th Gloucesters, died 16 July, 1916, aged twenty-three), Private George Knight (3rd South Wales Borderers, 16 August, 1918), Pioneer Ernest Mason (Royal Engineers, forty-three, 26 July, 1919), Sergeant George Henry Thomas (3rd Welsh Regiment, twenty-seven, 3 November, 1918) and Private Herbert Walding (Army Service Corps, 25 October, 1918). Also commemorated at family graves, but buried elsewhere, are Lance-Corporal Frederick John Brain, Fred Drivers and - the headstone draped with a rifle and sling - Sapper A. Harris.

On the drive up to The Forest Church, you would have noticed on the corner of the A4136 and Trinity Road, a plain stone cross. To reach this on foot, walk south-west through the churchyard until you reach a gate. Through this and you are now in the small memorial garden with its simple cross and inscription "We Remember".

ENGLISH BICKNOR - GLOUCESTERSHIRE

St. Mary's

Partly surrounded by Offa's Dyke, once the frontier between England and Wales, Gloucestershire's English Bicknor looks across the Wye to Welsh Bicknor in the neighbouring county of Herefordshire. The Gloucestershire village being found three miles to the north of Coleford.

The present St. Mary's was built c1100 – the churchyard is of Saxon origin – and its war memorial can be found close to the font on the south aisle. Look at its fine colours, sadly in need of restoration in places at time of writing (August, 2002), but in the main the reds, blues, greens, enhanced by gleaming gold, still look sharp and as bright as the day that they were first painted in the 1920s. And in the centre, the figure of Christ on the Cross surrounded by red roses and the rays of a golden sun.

Look now to the six names recorded on the memorial. At the top we see Kenneth Curling Doddrell (the vicar at St. Mary's was the Rev. Curling Finzel Doddrell) who was killed in Palestine on 19 September, 1918 while serving with

In fine reds, blues, greens and gold, the memorial at St. Mary's, English Bicknor still bright after more than eighty years.

the 1/4th Wiltshire Regiment. From that battalion's records (*The 1/4th Battalion The Wiltshire Regiment 1914-1919* by Lieutenant George Blick) we learn that the death took place during the attack at El Tireh - an important Turkish stronghold that featured in the "Big Push" of 19 September - but just hours prior to that Kenneth is mentioned in connection with the fighting some two miles away at Miskeh: "Lieutenant Doddrell, with No. 14 Platoon and others, were sent into the village of Miskeh on our left. Here our men surprised and took prisoner nearly 100 Turks, some of whom had only just been awakened from sleep, and the personnel of a Field Ambulance, complete with patients."

Of those that follow Kenneth Doddrell, records show that twenty-two-year-old Lance-Corporal Colin Eric Baumgarte (2/8th Worcestershire Regiment) was killed on the Western Front on 19 August, 1917; Lance-Corporal Ivor Victor Jones (11th Worcestershire Regiment) fell in Salonika on 24 April, 1917 (he was just nineteen and his parents lived at Millway Cottage, English Bicknor); Corporal Frederick Percy Adams ("K" Heavy Battery, Royal Garrison Artillery), France, 15 March, 1918 and Private Martin Powell (7th Gloucestershire Regiment), Mesopotamia, 25 February, 1917 - he was twenty-two. So far it has not been possible to establish, from the many W.J. Williams recorded among the dead of the First World War, the identity of the last name on the St. Mary's memorial.

Two names not mentioned on the memorial are those of Private Daniel William Davies and Forewoman F.M. Tooby. Both saw service in the First World War and occupy war graves in St. Mary's churchyard. Daniel Davies was twenty-two when he died from wounds on 3 February, 1916 - wounds probably received while serving with the 2nd Royal Marine Battalion at Gallipoli. His mother (Hannah), in the years that followed the war, is on record as living at Hillersland, just to the south-west of English Bicknor, and his wife (Lily May) at Mordiford near Hereford.

On the east side of the churchyard we see the grave of twenty-four-year-old F.M. Tooby - a relation possibly of local farmers Frank Tooby (Cowmeadow Farm) or Walter Charles Tooby (Eastbach Farm). A cook with the Queen Mary's Army Auxiliary Corps who must have been serving away from home in Woolwich when she died there at No. 73 Auxiliary Hospital on 14 November, 1918.

EWYAS HAROLD - HEREFORDSHIRE

Memorial Hall

Off the A465, approximately half way along the Hereford-Abergavenny road, lies Ewyas Harold. This deriving from an ancient name for the area and the early lordship of Harold of Ewyas. Shortly before reaching the village centre will be found the Memorial Hall. Erected in 1955 to the memory of those from the Ewyas Harold, Kenderchurch, Kentchurch and Dulas areas that laid-down their lives in both world wars. Mounted on wood, a brass tablet to the left just inside the entrance being given by members and friends of the Pontrilas District Branch of the Royal British Legion.

St. Michael's

Nancy Hall, in her history of Ewyas Harold Church, notes how situated in the Valley of the Dulas Brook, St. Michael's is an ancient building. Nothing of which remains dates earlier than the thirteenth century. Restored in 1868, the church now comprises chancel, nave, vestry and a western tower, thought to have been detached from the church at one time.

Memorial Hall, Ewyas Harold.

Entering through the south porch, to the right of the chancel arch lies the Standard of the Pontrilas and District Royal British Legion. Close by, an oval plaque bearing the date 1950 commemorates the dead of 1914-1918 and 1939-1945 - then to the right, a small framed Roll of Honour. This handwritten and listing the names of those that fell during the Great War: Ernest James Brown - Robert Dunkeld - John Reginald Jennings - Jeffrey George Povey - Thomas Valentine Price and Sidney Williams.

Born at Walford, Herefordshire, Lance-Corporal Ernest Brown was killed on 11 April, 1917 while serving in France with the 10th Royal Welsh Fusiliers. Sapper Robert Dunkeld, from Cummertrees, Dumfrieshire, and enlisting into the Royal Engineers at Hereford, would die on 26 January, 1917 from wounds received.

Private Jeffrey George Povey, thirty-two when he died on 22 August, 1917, is commemorated on the Tyne Cot Memorial to those who fell in the Ypres Salient during the period 1917-1918 and have no known graves. Serving with the 5th King's Shropshire Light Infantry, Private Povey on 22 August took part in an action to the east of Ypres. A successful operation that saw the Shropshires hold their gains until relieved during the night of 23-24 August. Casualties were high, however, and total one hundred and forty-four killed, wounded or missing.

Also with the King's Shropshire Light Infantry was Sergeant Thomas Valentine Price. Having left Palestine, the 10th KSLI arrived at Marseilles on 7 May, 1918 and during the second week of July was holding trenches at St. Floris - south of the La Lys Canal. A fairly quiet sector, records Major W. de B. Wood in his history of the KSLI, but "On the 29th the enemy attempted a raid. The 10th KSLI withheld fire until the enemy was right up to their trench line, when they let go and annihilated the raiding party. Unfortunately Sgt. T.V. Price, the best shot in the battalion, was killed in this affray." Tom Price is buried at St. Venant-Robecq Road British Cemetery. The Commonwealth War Graves Commission register there recording that he was thirty- years-old and the husband of Sylvia Emilie Price of Clehonger, Herefordshire.

Nancy Hall also notes in her book how the heating and lighting at St. Michael's has been improved from time to time. Electricity having been installed as a memorial to parishioners that lost their lives in both world wars.

Moving now to the south side of the churchyard we find another of those listed on the Roll of Honour. Private John Reginald Jennings being buried there after his death on 6 January, 1918. Aged eighteen and from Pontrilas, he had recently joined the South Lancashire Regiment and was serving with the 4th (Reserve) Battalion (Headquarters, Warrington) when he died. Listed in *Jaceman &*

Carvers Directory and Gazetteer of Herefordshire for 1914, the Jennings family are shown as plumbers, glaziers and painters.

The Lewis family, George and Minnie, are also buried in St. Michael's churchyard. Their headstone north of the church also remembering the death in Egypt on 4 August, 1916 of their son (whose name does not appear on the Roll) Sergeant William Edward Lewis. On this day the Battle of Romani opened, the Herefordshire Regiment being bombed by aeroplanes - followed by heavy artillery fire - before engaging with the Turkish infantry.

EYE - HEREFORDSHIRE

St. Peter and St. Paul

On the A49, just over three miles north of Leominster, turn left onto the minor road that leads down to Berrington Hall. A short distance past the entrance to this eighteenth-century house (now owned by the National Trust) you enter Eye. Its church, the south side dating from c1190, laying to the left of the road and opposite a cemetery extension.

Passing through the lych-gate - this having the words "In his care thy dead shall sleep" carved into the outer cross-beam - you find the first of two parish memorials. A stone tablet set into the brickwork and commemorating twenty-two men that lost their lives in the First World War, together with three from the Second. Proceeding the names, the dedication: "To the glory of God and in grateful remembrance of those from this parish who gave their lives for their country in the two world wars." In 1914 the Parish of Eye encompassed three other villages, Morton and Ashton to the east, Luston to the south-west.

Entering SS Peter and St. Paul on the north side of the church, the second parish memorial can be seen just inside the door to the left. Grey marble this time and with a similar inscription to that within the lych-gate. Notice here the first three names. Those of the Cawley brothers, sons of Lord and Lady Cawley who's home - Berrington Hall - was seen on the drive up to Eye.

Move now along the aisle (thirteenth century this part of the church) and enter the north chapel. The Cawley family prayed here, three of their four sons now commemorated on a fine marble memorial high-up on the wall. Depicted in true heraldic colours, the family Arms (three white swans on a black background, surmounted by a red rose between two blue garbs of wheat) look down onto a central tablet bearing the dedication. This including names, ranks, regiments, dates

Oswald Cawley.   *John Cawley.*   *Harold Cawley.*

and places of death, ages and where buried. There are two supporters. To the left, one holds a flambeau (flaming torch) reversed (the symbol of death), and to the right, another has (representing immortality) a lamp with flame.

Born at Crumpsall, Lancashire on 27 October, 1879, Major John Stephen Cawley was a regular soldier. Obtaining his Commission at the Royal Military College, Sandhurst and joining his regiment, the 20th Hussars, at Mhow, India in 1897. After South Africa (where, as Signalling Officer to General Low's Column he took part in operations in Orange River Colony and Cape Colony) he subsequently served in Egypt. Back home later (having passing through the Staff College) he was appointed Instructor at the Cavalry School, Netheravon in 1911, and in the following year he joined the General Staff at the War Office. He became Brigade Major to the 1st Cavalry Brigade in 1913 and it was as such that he sailed for France in August, 1914.

Killed on 1 September during the retirement from Mons, a brother officer gave the following account of John Cawley's death: "Our Brigade was attacked soon after dawn at Nery by a force double our number – a Cavalry Division with 12 guns. Owing to thick mist they managed to get within 600 yards of us; 350 horses of the Bays stampeded and their men went after them, and the 'L' Battery was cut to pieces. The occasion was one which called for personal example, and Major Cawley, by permission of the General, went to help to restore order and get the broken remnants in their places. The Situation being met and everyone being in his place, he joined the advance line and was almost immediately killed by a piece of shell. The splendid manner in which he met his death in deliberately facing the awful fire to help others when he really need not have done so, is only what his whole life has led us to expect." (This taken from Volume 1 of *The Bond of Sacrifice*.)

Major John Stephen Cawley is buried at Nery Communal Cemetery which he shares with the men of "L" Battery, Royal Horse Artillery and his brother Oswald. Interred there after his death in August, 1918. A good all-round sportsman, he played polo for his regiment, and at the 1905 Royal Military Tournament, took the Officers' riding and jumping prize.

The second son, Captain Harold Thomas Cawley, was born on 12 June, 1878 at Crumpsall, Lancashire. He went to Rugby School in 1891 and from there, in 1895, up to New College, Oxford. Graduating with honours from the History School, he left Oxford and was subsequently called to the Bar at the Inner Temple in 1902. Eight years later, and in the general election of January, 1910, he was returned as Liberal member for the south-east Lancashire Division of Heywood.

Harold Cawley's military career had began in 1904 when in that year he joined the 2nd Volunteer Battalion, Manchester Regiment. A keen horseman, he would be one of several officers attached to the battalion's "Mounted Infantry" Company. Briton's part-time soldiers, the Volunteer Force in 1908 became the Territorial Force - the 2nd VB Manchester at that time being redesignated as 6th Battalion.

August, 1914 saw Harold Cawley, MP, at the Home Office and serving as Secretary to the Rt. Hon. Reginald McKenna. War declared, he immediately volunteered for foreign service and with the Manchesters subsequently sailed for Egypt on 10 September, 1914. Captain Cawley - having been appointed Aide-de-Camp to Major-General W. Douglas, then GOC, 42nd (East Lancashire) Division - landed at Gallipoli early in May, 1915.

Turning now to the Rugby School Memorial Book, we learn that as ADC, Harold Cawley was not content with the comparative safety of Divisional Headquarters and requested that he be posted to his battalion in the forward area ("I have always felt rather a brute skulking behind in comparative safety while my friends were being killed..."). Most of the 6th Manchester officers had in fact been killed or wounded (including four old friends from Rugby) during the 4-5 June assault on Turkish positions at Krithia. His wish granted, he joined his men early in September - but in less than two weeks would himself be killed. The following accounts of his short service in the front line appeared in *Memorials of Rugbeians who fell in the Great War Volume II*:

(1) "When we went up to the front line I put him in charge of the firing trench, and it was due in a great measure to his coolness and bravery, on the day that we had a very large mine blown up just against our trench, that the men were quite cool, every one in his place, and ready, if there had been a Turkish attack." (*Commanding Officer*)

(2) "He obtained leave to join the tattered remnants of the regiment which he loved more than life. He knew the full cost of it, the almost inevitable end, and he deliberately accepted that cost without a moment's hesitation or regret." (*The Rt. Hon. C.F.C. Masterman*)

(3) "Captain Cawley was a very brave and unassuming gentleman; one of his exploits is worth recounting. A small ammunition cart had been taken up the principal nullah, where the men proceeded to unload in order to carry the cases to the dug-out. The enemy spotted this waggon and immediately started to shell it vigorously with shrapnel. Naturally there was a slight hesitancy on the part of the men unloading as to what was the wisest thing to do. Captain Cawley settled the situation by getting off his horse into the cart and handing the boxes down in double-quick time. After the vehicle was clear he coolly rode away." (*"A Manchester Territorial"*)

Age thirty-seven, Harold Thomas Cawley was buried at Lancashire Landing Cemetery. This place overlooking "W" Beach - scene of the 1st Lancashire Fusiliers landing on 25 April, 1915.

A Member of Parliament since 1895, Sir Frederick Cawley was elevated to the peerage on 16 January, 1918. His son, Oswald, being immediately invited to contest his father's seat at Prestwich, Lancashire. He was subsequently elected by a large majority, even though his stipulation - whereas he remained away from home on active service - was upheld.

Oswald Cawley also went to Rugby School and Oxford. Working in his father's business (the Heaton Mills Bleaching Company) before travelling around the world in 1911. He joined the Shropshire Yeomanry in May, 1914 and in March, 1916 went to Egypt. Here the regiment served with the Baharia Field Force and in November, 1916 entered Palestine. After the fighting for Gaza and Jerusalem, the Yeomanry (now designated as 10th King's Shropshire Light Infantry) left for France on 1 May, 1918. A period of training was carried out at St. Hilaire, then on 10 July a section of the front line at St. Flois was taken over - the battalion's line running between the Lys Canal and St. Venant-Merville Railway. A "fairly quiet sector" notes regimental historian of the KSLI - Major W. de B. Wood.

On 22 August, however, orders were received to move forward. A general advance being made north of the canal. The attack, records Major Wood "....was unfortunately hung up, and, without any information of the position on the left flank, the 10th KSLI proceeded into what proved to be for them a trap. Advancing through high standing corn the battalion continued until within a few hundred yards of the concealed enemy, who met them with a devastating fire......He then followed up his advantage with a determined counter-attack and severe hand-to-hand fighting took place."

Further details (published in *Memorials of Rugbeians who fell in the Great War*) were received in a letter sent by the 10th KSLI Commanding Officer to Lord and Lady Cawley: "Your son's company was on the right....The enemy lay low, until we were right on their line, and then put down a very heavy barrage behind us and had many machine guns in front..... Your son was hit in the arm, which he got dressed by his Company stretcher-bearers, and then went on and was wounded again the second time in the jaw, and after that we could hear no news, and we had to fall back to our old line." Captain Oswald Cawley was subsequently buried close to his brother at Nery Communal Cemetery.

There are five war graves in the churchyard at SS Peter and Paul. Four having the standard Commonwealth War Graves Commission headstone, and one, a private marker bearing a cross. All are located to the east of the church. The four CWGC graves are those of: Driver Charles Beech (Royal Field Artillery), who died 8 December, 1919; Private George Frederick Gardner (10th South Wales Borderers), twenty-three when he died on 11 November, 1920 and the son of George Gardner (a sexton from Luston); Private Harry Mantell (Herefordshire Regiment), died 2 February, 1916 aged twenty-seven and Lance-Corporal Thomas James Mutlow (3rd Herefordshire Regiment) who died of phthisis on 5 July, 1916. He was twenty-three and came from Morton.

The inscription on the last and private headstone notes that Angus Campbell was the only son of Alex and Mary Campbell (Provost of Lochgair). His age is given as just fifteen. From Luston, Mrs Campbell is recorded in the 1914 edition of *Jackman & Carver's Directory And Gazetteer Of Herefordshire* as a grocer. Turning now to the records held by the CWGC, we note that Angus Woodhouse Campbell served with the 1/st Herefordshire Regiment and died of sickness on 21 February, 1915. *Soldiers Died In The Great War* giving place of birth as Lochgair, Argyllshire.

GANAREW - HEREFORDSHIRE

St. Swithin's

The south Herefordshire village of Ganarew is on the A466, three miles north-east of Monmouth and close to the border with Monmouthshire. In the church, which dates from 1850, the reredos forms the village war memorial - a fine sculpture in white marble that features the figure of Christ with hands outstretched and accompanied by two Angels. To the right, and on the south wall of the chancel, a stone tablet notes that it was erected there by the relatives and friends of the six men that fell, and close by a framed list dated 1926 provides a record of those that subscribed. The memorial is also intended as a thanks offering for those who were spared.

In his contribution to Colonel J.M. Findlay's book *With The 8th Scottish Rifles*, Captain W. Whigham Ferguson, MC records how on 30 July, 1918, when he resumed command of "Y" Company after an attack at Beugneux, he had found that all his officers had been lost. What remained of the Company being then under the control of just three NCOs. Before a second attack could take place on 1 August, reinforcements were desperately required. These, notes Captain Ferguson, arriving in the darkness just two hours prior to "zero" and in the form of Captain Donald Clark Johnston and Lieutenant Hardie. The latter had not been in action, and to both officers, Captain Ferguson set out the plan: "I explained the position to them by the failing light of an 'orilux' electric lamp, with the aid of a map and sketches. Four hours later, when the objective was reached, it was my sad experience to find that both these officers were casualties, Captain Johnston having paid the full sacrifice, and Lieut. Hardie being wounded.

The advance, records the battalion's records, commenced at 4.15 am, and had taken place in dense fog, shell-smoke and clouds of mustard gas. Confusion inevitable, notes Captain Ferguson, but despite a stiff fight by the enemy, Hill 158 was taken and "we got a goodly bag of Boche, including machine-guns."

During August, 1917 the 7th King's Shropshire Light Infantry were holding trenches in the Frémicourt sector and it was in this month that the battalion war diary notes the arrival of Second-Lieutenant Alfred James Norris. On 26 September, the battalion, now in the Ypres area, took part in the Battle of Polygon Wood - a successful operation that saw both German first and second lines occupied.

When the German Spring Offensive began on 21 March, 1918, the 7th KSLI were holding trenches in the Hindenburg Line west of Héninel. Here, until

Grave of Sapper and railwayman William James Goodwin, St. Swithin's churchyard, Garnarew. Through the horrors of the war in France and Flanders - but to die from its effects at home.

relieved on the 28th, they would suffer casualties numbering fifty-four killed, one hundred and eighty-three wounded, one hundred and sixty missing. Twenty-two-year-old Alfred Norris, originally among the latter, was later confirmed as having been killed on 28 March. He has no known grave.

Mobilization on 4 August, 1914 saw the immediate departure, for Cork in Ireland, of No. 1 Siege Company, Royal Monmouthshire Royal Engineers (Militia). Soon, Nos. 2 and 3 Companies were on the move from their Regimental Headquarters in Monmouth, but on this occasion Longmoor, Hampshire would be the destination - where for the early weeks of the war the men would carry out their duties as Railway Troops. A move to France was made on 10 November, 1914, where (as well as in Flanders) various types of construction work was performed. Serving with No. 2 (Railway) Company, Sapper William James Goodwin is one of five men recorded in the regiment's records as a "fatal casualty"

- dying at home as a result of shell-shock on 11 April, 1917. His body was buried in the churchyard at St. Swithin's.

Initially serving with the Hereford-based Welsh Divisional Army Service Corps (Territorial Force), Rifleman Henry Goodwin was later transferred to the 1/18th London Regiment. This better known as the "London Irish Rifles". He was then posted to the 9th Royal Irish Rifles, and subsequently killed during the fighting at Cambrai on 23 November, 1917.

Although the St. Swithin's memorial gives Rifleman Alfred George Morris's initials as "A.J.", he is shown in William Collings's book *Herefordshire And The Great War* as Alfred George. His regiment is confirmed as the King's Royal Rifle Corps, and the War Office records (*Soldiers Died In The Great War*) show that he was serving with the 18th Battalion when he was killed on 31 July, 1917. The battalion on that day holding positions in the sub-sector south of the Ypres-Commines Canal and attacking the enemy's line at Hollebeke. Moving forward through mist, drizzling rain and thick deep mud, the progress of the 18th KRRC was slow - the enemy taking full advantage and pouring machine gun fire into the oncoming troops.

The 1/1st Herefordshire Regiment had left Egypt for France on 17 June, 1918 and on 1 July, 1918 joined the recently reconstructed 34th Division at Bambecque. Private Edward Jones was killed on the following 5 September, the battalion then holding part of the line near Wytschaete.

GLOUCESTER

Cathedral

Appointed by William the Conqueror as Abbot of Gloucester in 1072, the Norman monk Serlo around 1086 began building a new abbey. This to replace that founded c681 as an Anglo-Saxon monastery dedicated to St. Peter. Consecrated in July, 1100 - it is most of this building that survives today - it would achieve cathedral status after the dissolution of the monasteries in 1536 and upon the subsequent establishment of the new diocese of Gloucester in September, 1541.

To see the cathedral's several First World War memorials, begin by walking along the north aisle. To the left of the organ - its decorated pipework dominating the centre of the nave - there are two plaques situated, one left and one right, of a doorway. On the left, a brass plaque tells how in 1920, and in memory of their youngest son, Sir James and Lady Horlick reconstructed and enlarged the organ. This work being carried out by Messrs. Harrison & Harrison.

Major Gerald Nolekin Horlick was born Brooklyn, New York in February, 1888 and having been educated at Eton and Brasenose College, Oxford, later became Assistant Works Manager in the family business at Slough, Bucks - the famous Horlick's Malted Milk Company. He had been a officer in the Royal Gloucestershire Hussars Yeomanry since 1907 (see RGH section below).

As its Machine Gun Officer, Gerald Horlick left with his regiment for Egypt on 11 April, 1915 and later, from Madros (the advanced base for the Gallipoli campaign), crossed to the peninsular via the paddle steamer *Queen Victoria* (formerly of the Isle of Man service) on 17 August. His subsequent service, both at Gallipoli and later in Egypt and Palestine, where he became attached to the Cavalry Machine Gun Corps as

Regimental cap badge, and Back Badge (proudly earned in Egypt and Korea) of the Gloucesters, War Memorial Chapel, Gloucester Cathedral.

Commanding Officer, was highly regarded. A brother officer wrote of him: "He was not only respected by all as a Commanding Officer, but also loved as a friend by everybody; we all feel that his place will never be filled. It seems hard that he should die in this way after having gone through so many battles unhurt. It was devotion to duty that made him remain with the squadron in the Jordan Valley when he was not really fit to do so." Mentioned in Despatches by General Sir Charles Munro (*London Gazette* 10 October, 1916) and again by General Sir Edmund Allenby (*London Gazette* 3 April, 1918) for gallant and distinguished service in the field, Gerald Horlick would die from malaria at No.17 General Hospital, Alexandria on 5 July, 1918.

Next, look to the right of the doorway and the plaque here remembers poet, composer and songwriter, Ivor Gurney. Surviving the war for almost twenty years, only to die from its terrible effects in 1937. More of this "....lover and maker of beauty" (from his headstone) at St. Matthew's, Twigworth.

Continue now along the north side, passing many old Colours of the Gloucestershire Regiment, and in the north transept is the White Ensign flown by HMS *Gloucester* during the First World War. Built by Beardmore in 1909, this light cruiser took part in the hunt for the *Emden* in November, 1914, captured the German supply ship *Macedonia*, February, 1915 and in the following year would shell Galway during the Easter Uprising. Service in the Adriatic and East Indies followed.

Having reached the north ambulatory (this dating from the last decade of the eleventh century) we find St. Edmund and St. Edward's Chapel. Known also as the War Memorial Chapel and including glazed cabinets containing hand-written memorial books to the dead

Nine Freemasons remembered in the cloisters at Gloucester Cathedral.

of Gloucestershire - and in particular two regiments. The Gloucestershire Regiment and Royal Gloucestershire Hussars Yeomanry. Note the regimental badges, these repeated again in a window above, along with words telling how some eight thousand, one hundred from the Gloucestershire Regiment alone were killed.

At the extreme east end of the cathedral we find the Lady Chapel. Completed c1500 and including, just inside the entrance on the right, an illuminated Roll of Honour commemorating pupils of the King's School, Gloucester who fell in two world wars. There are thirty recorded for 1914-1918 and twenty-six for 1939-1945.

Move back now to the west end and almost directly opposite the cathedral entrance is the doorway leading to the cloisters. Not far along the north walk we come to the first of two interesting memorials. A bronze plaque set into the wall and in memory of nine Freemasons from the Gloucestershire area who were killed: Cyril Winterbottom, Harold Organ, Michael Quenington, Evelyn Pearson, Robert Anderson, Basil Bruton, Robert Jones, Herbert Owen and Herbert Tedder.

On the Somme, the 1/5th Gloucestershire Regiment had returned to the front line on 25 August, 1916. The battalion's position being at Donnets Post - Lieutenant Cyril William Winterbottom commanding "C" Company near points referred to in the battalion war diary as "X2" and "C38" (these being communication trenches leading from the support to firing line). In the attack made on 27 August, Cyril Winterbottom would lose his life while leading his men into the German front line. A determined and successful assault in which "....so eager were the men to attack that 'C' Company were among the enemy before the British guns had lifted" (Wyrall). With no known grave, Lieutenant Winterbottom's name appears on the Thiepval Memorial to the missing of the Somme.

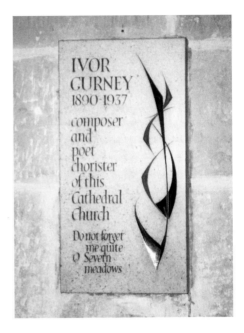

"Lover and maker of beauty" - Ivor Gurney memorial, Gloucester Cathedral.

At the beginning of November, 1917, the 1/5th Gloucestershire Regiment was holding a sector of the British line immediately in front of Vimy Ridge - a very quiet area notes the historian of the 48th Division, Lieutenant-Colonel George Henry Barnett, CMG, DSO. But with news of the Italian disaster at Caporetto, orders were soon received directing the 48th (with 1/5 Gloucesters) to that theatre of war. Leaving on 24 November, the battalion arrived by train at Montagnana on the morning of the 29th.

The battalion war diary notes the return from leave on 4 June, 1918 of Captain Basil Vassal Bruton. Five days later the Gloucesters took over front line trenches at Carriola, then on 15 June a single-line entry reads: "Enemy Attack." Reading Major P.A. Hall's "Narrative of Operations" for that day we learn that the enemy, before his infantry came on in great numbers, had opened a heavy bombardment of gas and high explosive shells about 2.45 am. Turning now to Colonel Barnett's history we hear that "The 1/5th Gloucesters found their left company taken in enfilade and reverse, and it was almost surrounded.....counter-attacks by two platoons and the support company were unable to hold up the enemy advance...." What was left of the battalion was eventually able to withdraw - its casualties totalling two hundred and twenty-one killed, missing or wounded. One of the latter, Captain Basil Bruton would later succumb to his wounds and be buried in Boscon British Cemetery on the Asiago Plateau. The register for which notes that his parents were Henry and Flora of Gloucester, and that he was the husband of Isabel Frances Stewart Bruton of 88 London Road.

The Freemason's memorial has another member of the Gloucestershire Regiment. This time the Bristol-based 1/4th Battalion and Lieutenant Harold Charles Organ. Coincidentally a Fellow of the Royal College of Organists and one time deputy at Gloucester Cathedral. Killed during the 9 October, 1917 Battle of Polelcapelle, he went into action that day shortly after 4.30 am. The battalion had come up to the forward area in buses the evening before and were to attack the strongly held German position known as Oxford House. "Immediately the advance commenced our men" (Operation Report) "came under machine gun fire....snipers were also very active...." Just a few men managed to get near their objective - but these were soon compelled to fall back. Total casualties: one hundred and seventy-seven killed, wounded or missing. Harold was twenty-eight and his parents lived at 25 Brunswick Square, Gloucester.

Turning now to the Royal Gloucestershire Hussars Yeomanry, we have two officers: Captain Michael Hugh Viscount Quenington, killed in action Egypt, 23 April, 1916 and Lieutenant Robert Graham Anderson who fell at Balin, Palestine on 12 November, 1917.

Also to serve with a yeomanry regiment was Herbert Edgar Tedder. A trooper with the 1st North Somerset who died from wounds received on 29 November, 1914. From its headquarters at Bath, the Regiment had landed in France three weeks before (3 November) and on the 13th joined the 6th Cavalry Brigade - then holding trenches on the Ypres Salient. Part of 6th Brigade was the 3rd Dragoon Guards whose regimental history (Holt) tells how on "The previous day [13 November] the North Somerset Yeomanry had marched in from Dranoutre...With two squadrons... they [3rd Dragoon Guards] then took over trenches on the eastern side of the Zillebeke-Klein Zillebeke road..." Although under almost continuous shell and rifle fire, the Yeomen would see their first major action on 17 November. The Prussian Guard opposite making a determined attack shortly after 9 am - this being repulsed by dusk. "The North Somerset Yeomanry.... behaved very gallantly. They had 2 Officers and 21 Other Ranks killed and 1 Officer and 27 Other Ranks wounded."

We turn now to the 12th King's (Liverpool Regiment) and the death on 8 January, 1916 of Captain Evelyn Henry Malcolm Paterson Pearson. Forty-one when he was killed in trenches near Fleurbaix in France. His battalion had been in France since 27 July, 1915. Then we have Second-Lieutenant Herbert Morris Owen, wounded while serving with the 9th Cheshire Regiment. He would die in hospital at Amiens on 25 March, 1918 and be buried at St. Pierre Cemetery (on the Albert Road just to the north-west of the city).

Lieutenant Robert Nelson Jones of the 4th Northamptonshire Regiment (latter Machine Gun Corps) has no known grave. Killed on 31 July, 1917, his name also appears on the Menin Gate Memorial at Ypres.

On now to the east side, and there to the right of the Chapter House door, another bronze. This time in memory of a single officer, Second-Lieutenant Raymond Edward Knight, and erected - along with the installation of electric lighting in the Chapter House and that of the Great Cloister - by his brother in 1928.

It would be as Corporal Knight that Raymond was awarded the Distinguished Conduct Medal while in France. The war diary of his unit - 1/5th Gloucestershire Regiment - recording this on 26 August, 1915 and mentioning that he, along with F.W. Harvey, had been given the award "For consistent good patrolling." Frederick William Harvey - poet and friend of Ivor Gurney - being from Minsterworth.

Receiving his commission (dated 16 October, 1915), Second-Lieutenant Knight returned to France from England and re-joined the 1/5th Gloucesters (posted to "B" Company) at Couin on the Somme 24 June, 1916. Two days before his death, on 21 July, 1916, the 1/5th Gloucesters took over front line trenches north-east of Ovillers. Here the battalion was to take part in a number of "local" attacks, these with a view to pushing forward their division's - the 46th (North Midland) - line in this sector. By 11 pm (19 July) the first assault (led by "B" Company) had taken place - but their objective fiercely defended a withdrawal was forced. This was the case next day, and again on the 21st when, having been mortally wounded, Raymond Knight died.

Also to be considered along with the cathedral - its location being on College Green near to the west door - is the regimental memorial unveiled by Lieutenant-General P.W. Chetwode, Bt, KCB, KCMG, DSO on 29 April, 1922. "In memory of the members of the Royal Gloucestershire Hussars Yeomanry who gave up their lives in the Great War 1914-1918" is the dedication carved into the stone-work of the eight-sided super base - "....entirely a regimental memorial...." - the committee responsible having - "....secured all the funds required from relatives of the fallen and members and ex-members of the regiment....(no public subscriptions having been solicited)" (Fox).

The monument comprises three steps - these leading up to an eight-sided sub-base on which are mounted eight bronze panels. On four (the larger) scenes representing the regiment's four years of war service appear in low-relief, their titles being - "Salt Lake to Chocolate Hill" (Gallipoli, 1915); "The sand of the desert" (Sinai, 1916); "Crossing the Jordan" (Palestine, 1917) and "Watering the horses" (Syria, 1918). The remaining and narrower panels take the form of a Roll of Honour and records names and ranks of the two hundred and twenty-nine yeoman that died. These arranged in alphabetically order and with no attention to rank.

One of four fine bronze panels from the Royal Gloucestershire Hussars Yeomanry memorial on College Green, Gloucester.

The Royal Gloucestershire Hussars were part of Britain's Territorial Force and as part-time soldiers - existing essentially as a means of home defence - were not required to serve overseas. At the outbreak of war in August, 1914 the regiment comprised four squadrons and was located: Headquarters Gloucester; "A" Squadron - Gloucester (with detachments at Ledbury, Cheltenham and Winchcombe); "B" Squadron - Stroud (with detachments at Westonbirt, Yate, Berkely, Cirencester and Bourton-on-the-water); "C" Squadron - Newport, Monmouthshire (with detachments at Cardiff, Chepstow, Ebbw Vale, Monmouth and Abergavenny) and "D" Squadron - Bristol (detachments at Broadmead, Tockington and Horfield). But on 11 April, 1915 the regiment, three squadrons strong and made up of volunteers, left Avonmouth for Egypt. Its subsequent war service and contribution in lives lost being told in their fine memorial.

St. Mary de Crypt

In Southgate Street, the Norman church of St. Mary de Crypt (key available at the Tourist Information Office opposite) is always worth a visit when in Gloucester. On the north side, a stone screen at the entrance to a chapel has the words above: "To the glory of God and in grateful memory of the fallen 1914-1918." On the panels below there are thirty-two names carved into the stonework.

Formed at St. Mary's in 1539 was the Crypt School. Now at Podsmead, on the southern outskirts of Gloucester, and with a fine memorial of its own.

HEREFORD

All Saints

At the northern end of Bond Street in the city centre, All Saints spire of two hundred and twenty-five feet (with those of the cathedral and St. Peter's) dominates the Hereford skyline. Medieval, this church of fine woodwork and glass (about 1220 says the guidebook) – but now very much part of the twenty-first century. Enjoy the new café – opened in July, 1997 and "....skilfully fitted into the medieval fabric to serve the human need for physical as well as spiritual nourishment."

Designed by Hereford architect William Clarke (of Nicholson & Clarke) a hanging rood would be chosen by the parish as its war memorial. This installed in 1921 and including – in the south chapel close to the fifteenth-century screen – an oak panel bearing in gold letters the names of the eighty-two that were killed. Note the delicately-carved gallery at the top of the memorial.

In the same chapel, another memorial – this time in marble and that moved from the Hereford School for Boys to All Saints in 1986. With an average age of nineteen, the six Old Boys recorded were surely still at school when war broke out in 1914. All of them losing their lives within the last eight months of the war.

Private Edward Hedley Caffyn of the 1st Grenadier Guards and youngest son of George and Deborah Caffyn of College Buildings, 137 Widemarch Street, Hereford. The first to die (3 April, 1918) – his battalion that day holding trenches at Boisleux-au-Mont where (notes the unit war diary) the enemy were "....showing very little signs of life." This could not be said in the case of Private William George Drew's battalion, the 1/4th East Yorkshires. Killed 1 June, 1918 as what remained of the unit (practically annihilated during the "Battle of the Aisne") fought in independent groups as they fell back to Fismes.

Private Leonard Wilkinson (5th Gordon Highlanders) also fell at the height of an important battle - Second Marne, 28 July, 1918. Then came Rifleman Peter Alexander Cowden, killed 18 September while serving with the 15th London Regiment (Civil Service Rifles), and on the same day the only one of the six not to lose his life on the Western Front. Private Frederick Jennings of 12 Elgin Street, Hereford being with the 8th King's Shropshire Light Infantry in Salonica.

The last Hereford High School former pupil to die was Corporal Herbert Waite Brooke of the 26th Royal Fusiliers who was killed 21 October, 1918. His battalion, with just weeks to go to the end of the war, operating west of the Courtrai-Bossuyt Canal on that day and coming under heavy artillery and machine gun fire as the went forward.

Before leaving All Saints look up to the Tudor roof over the south aisle. There carved into one of the spandrels - a medieval "flasher".

Cathedral

Entering Hereford's fine cathedral through its west door, immediately turn to face two splendid memorials - one either side of the doorway. To the left, the motto of the Herefordshire Regiment - *Manu Forti* (with a strong hand) - appears in gold below its cap badge (the crest from the Arms of Hereford) at the top of a finely-carved monument in white marble. At the bottom, another reminder of the county in the form of its apples and cider production. "Remembered in God" are the five hundred and twenty-two members of the regiment that fell during its service in 1914-1919. Service that can be summed-up by the four theatres of war engraved on the memorial, and its battle honours: "Marne, 1918" - "Soissonnais-Ourcq" - "Ypres, 1918" - "Courtrai" - "France and Flanders, 1918" - "Suvla" - "Landing at Suvla" - Scimitar Hill" - "Gallipoli, 1915" - "Rumani" - Egypt, 1916-17" - "Gaza" - "El Mughar" - "Jerusalem" - "Tell 'Asur" - "Palestine, 1917-18". Below the memorial a book of remembrance listing the names of those killed.

To the right of the doorway - his family Arms above, regimental crest (Grenadier Guards) below - the service of a single old soldier is set out in great detail within two black-shafted Ionic columns. A Member of Parliament since 1900, Captain Percy Archer Clive rejoined his old regiment at the outbreak of war and was soon out with the 2nd Battalion in France. Regarding a patrol that took place during the night of 18 February, 1915 while in the Guinchy sector, regimental historian Lieutenant-Colonel the Right Hon. Sir Frederick Ponsonby, records how that day the enemy had managed to take part of the line held by the French on the Grenadiers right. A French patrol was subsequently sent out to retake the position, but no report as to the success of the operation having been received, it was concluded that the lost trench could be in either French or German hands. In order to verify the situation, the French commander sent a reconnoitring party into the Grenadiers line and asked permission from Captain Clive to investigate the doubtful area. Offering his help, he actually led the French party – arriving in a dug-out that without doubt (there was German kit and a lighted candle burning) was occupied by the enemy. Then, insisting on making further investigation, Captain Clive ventured out into the pitch darkness: "Suddenly he was challenged in deep guttural German by a sentry, not two yards off. '*Français, Français*' he replied in a voice to which he was uncertain whether he should give a French or German

Family arms surmount the fine service record of Lieutenant-Colonel Percy Archer Clive at Hereford Cathedral.

accent, '*Holt Oder Ich Schiesse*', was the reply, and the nationality of the occupants of the trench was settled beyond dispute.....as the bullets whistled past him when he retired, the nationality of their makers was forcibly impressed on his mind."

Another lucky escape, this time on 6 August, 1915, occurred while Captain Clive was leading a working party. He and his men being just a short distance away when a German mine was exploded in their path. A number of the Grenadiers would be completely buried (one was killed, eighteen suffered severe shock and contusions) – Clive himself being badly cut and bruised by the mass of debris that was blown past him. Shot up into the air, he came down so doubled up that his teeth were nearly knocked out by his knees (Ponsonby).

As the memorial records, Captain (now temporary Lieutenant-Colonel) Clive, went on to command the 7th East Yorkshire Regiment. He served on the Somme in 1916, taking part in the opening battles, and would be wounded in the thigh and arm while visiting the front line near Lesboeufs on 3 November.

In the action at Bucquoy on 5 April, 1918, Colonel Clive, now commanding the 1/5th Lancashire Fusiliers, went forward with part of his battalion in counter-attack on the right. The village had been the scene of much hand-to-hand fighting and casualties among the assaulting troops were mounting. The advance having been held up at the Bucquoy cross-roads, records Major-General J.C. Latter, CBE, MC, "Sutton [Captain G.W. Sutton] went to reconnoitre but, while looking at his map, was seriously wounded. When Lieutenant-Colonel Clive heard of this, he brought forward some stretcher-bearers and came to Sutton to learn the situation on the front of the 1/8th [1/8th Battalion, Lancashire Fusiliers, Sutton in temporary command]. As he turned away after getting the information and ensuring that the

"With a strong hand" - Herefordshire Regiment memorial and Book of Honour, Hereford Cathedral.

stretcher-bearers had began to carry Sutton to the rear, he was killed." With no known grave, Lieutenant-Colonel Percy Archer Clive's name was placed on the Arras Memorial at Faubourg-d'Amiens Cemetery.

Four more individual soldiers are commemorated on the south side of the cathedral. First, and below the badge of the Devonshire Regiment, we see the name of Major Henry C. Carden - "A gallant soldier and a true friend" notes the inscription. This also establishing (from the date of birth and death provided) that he would be in his sixtieth year when he fell at the head of his men during the Battle of Loos.

An old soldier - he was awarded his Distinguished Service Order in South Africa, while serving in the Boer War - Henry Carden would play an important role in the formation and training of the 8th Devonshire Regiment. One of Kitchener's "New Army" battalions and made up entirely of volunteers. At one time the battalion thought that it was never to be called - one young officer wrote

"A gallant soldier and a true friend" remembered at Hereford Cathedral.

"Are they to keep us here for ever?" - but on 25 July, after having been in existence for almost a year, the turn of the 8th Devons came. Crossing to France that day - Henry Carden as its Second-in-Command.

It would be with little front line experience that the battalion moved into the forward area during the evening of 24 September, 1915. They, with the 9th Devons, were to attack Cite St. Elie, a heavily defended village which, from the British line, lay up a gentle slope fronted by the enemy's Breslau Trench. At 5.30 am on 25 September an intensive bombardment began - shell after shell descending on the German line for a solid hour - then "Zero". Charging forward the Devons went on, but from Breslau, the defenders lining their parapet poured a steady fire into them. Henry Carden being among the many to fall within the first minutes of the attack and never to be seen alive again.

Still in the south aisle, we move on to a group of three plaques situated close to the entrance of the cathedral shop and around a finley-carved brass commemorating those officer of the 36th Regiment (later 2nd Worcestershire) that died in India during its 1863-1875 tour.

An oak panel in the school library, but the names of eighty-five Old Boys of the Hereford Cathedral School in brass at Hereford Cathedral.

To the left another Herefordshire Regiment cap badge and a motto. The latter on this occasion being that of the city itself – *Invicta Fidelitas Præmiun* (the reward of invincible fidelity). An appropriate choice, the subject of the memorial having been Hereford born (26 August, 1875), educated at the Cathedral School and served the place well as Registrar of the County Court and Deputy and County Coroner. He was made a Freeman of the City.

Wilfrid Townshend Carless, also joined the local volunteers – the 1st Herefordshire Rifle Volunteer Corps which became the Herefordshire Regiment in 1908 – and since 1897 had served as one of its officers. It would be with the rank of major that Wilfrid Carless went to war in 1915, his memorial providing much information: "He sailed with the British Mediterranean Expeditionary Force to the Dardanelles on 16th July 1915, landed at Suvla Bay at dawn on August 9th, he was last seen in the evening of August 12th while in command of the battalion and has been 'missing' since that date."

For more detail of the events leading up to Wilfrid's death (his body was never found) we turn first to G. Archer Parfitt's *Historical Records of the Herefordshire Light Infantry and its Predecessors:* "The Herefords moved off by half Battalions at about 4.30pm [9 August]. Major Carless led with 'D' and 'C' Companies, and as soon as they topped the shoulder of Lala Baba, came under artillery fire. The two leading Companies extended and ploughed their way across rough ground which, for the most part, was covered with brush wood. After advancing for more than a mile some wounded men directed them....The last part of the journey was completely under hot rifle fire."

After nightfall, the situation had become confusing, the 53rd Division, in which the Herefords were serving, being "....scattered in all directions....the 158th Brigade had the Herefords in action southeast of Lala Baba...." (Dudley Ward). Contact with Major Carless lost, the battalion's commanding officer, Lieutenant-Colonel G. Dradge was himself wounded and taken to hospital. This passing command to Carless.

Back to the Western Front now and the death at Moen in Belgium on 21 October, 1918 of Corporal Herbert Waite Brooke - "Only son of Mr. H. Brooke of this Cathedral Choir....Aged 19....One of God's noblest sons, passed on to higher work" - notes his bronze plaque.

Born in Ipswich, Herbert Waite had originally enlisted into the 28th Royal Fusiliers. This battalion being a reserve formation providing and training recruits for the 18th and 19th Fusiliers - both made up of former public school and university men. He would, however, join the 26th Royal Fusiliers - also known as the "Bankers Battalion" and raised by the Lord Mayor and City of London in July, 1915 from bank clerks and accountants.

On the day of Herbert's death, the battalion war diary records simply "Active operations." But H.C. O'Neill gives a more detailed account: "....the 26th Battalion were operating west of the canal [Courtrai-Bossuyt]. The brigade [124th] moved forward about 11am towards the Laatse Oortie-Hoogstraatje Ridge....the 26th Royal Fusiliers were to move forward from support to the position vacated by the Queen's [10th Queen's Royal West Surrey Regiment] and then move forward to the Scheldt....unfortunately the troops had only reached the ridge when heavy artillery and machine-gun fire caught them from the east of the canal. The 26th Battalion could not advance, despite repeated efforts; and an attempt by D Company at night was also checked by unbroken wire and machine guns."

Just above Herbert Brooke's memorial is that to Lieutenant-Colonel Edward Bourryau Luard - this providing the following information: "....Who died on

Easter Monday April 24 1916 of wounds received on the night of Good Friday when the 1st Bn. K.S.L.I. (under his command) re-took the trenches on the Ypres-Langemarck road and was laid to rest in the cemetery nr Poperinghe." Erected by his wife, the plaque goes on to note that Edward Luard was "Adjutant of the 4th Bn. K.S.L.I. at Hereford 1902-1905 [a Militia battalion and the regiment's reserve]" and "Married in the Lady Chapel of this cathedral in 1905 to Louise, daughter of the Revd. Sidney Lidderdale Smith, Canon Residentiary of Hereford."

The son of Lieutenant-General R.G.A. Luard, Edward Luard was born 20 September, 1870. He was educated at Clifton College, then from Sandhurst entered the Army in May, 1891 - seeing service in South Africa, 1900-1902. In the Great War he was present at during the September, 1914 fighting on the Marne and at Armentières. On 28 January, 1916 he was sent to hospital suffering from the effects of gas. Awarded the Distinguished Service Order in 1915 "for services in connection with operations in the field", Edward Luard was twice Mentioned in Despatches. The cemetery near Poperinghe referred to on his memorial is at Lijssenthoek just to the south-west.

To the eastern end of the cathedral now and in the Lady Chapel a brass plaque - unveiled on 16 December, 1921 by the then Dean of Hereford, the Very Rev. R. W. Waterfield - records in alphabetical order below the school crest the names of sixty-nine former pupils of the Hereford Cathedral School that lost their lives. Some four hundred and eighty-five Old Boys of the school served in the Great War and an oak memorial board was also erected in the school library.

St. Peter's

Hereford's oldest church; St. Peter's was founded in about 1070 by Walter de Lacy (later to be killed by a fall from its roof) and rebuilt at the end of the twelfth or beginning of the thirteenth century. The chancel survives this period. Tower added (late thirteenth century), north aisle (c1300), south chapel and spire (fourteenth century).

Entering St. Peter's on the south side and descending some three feet (an indication as to how the street level has risen in nine hundred years, notes the church guidebook) turn to the left. Here on the south wall a fine carved oak panel commemorates forty-seven men of the parish that gave their lives in the First World War. Those that fell 1939-1945 are recorded in three panels below.

Note the names of the Daw brothers. George, thirty-four when he was killed on 18 June, 1917 while serving in France with the 7th King's Shropshire Light Infantry - the battalion that day taking over the defences at Monchy near Arras -

and younger brother thirty-three-year-old William who fell just over a month later on 25 July. The boys were the sons of Francis Daw - a fishmonger of 28/29 St. Owen Street, Hereford.

Another name is that of Eric Gwynne James - Captain and Adjutant of the 1st Battalion, King's Shropshire Light Infantry. Born 25 August, 1893, Eric James was the son of Hereford solicitor Francis Reginald James (Folly road, Aylestone hill) and was commissioned 15 August, 1914. He joined his battalion at Armentières in the following January, was appointed Adjutant in August, 1915, Mentioned in Despatches June, 1916 and later awarded the Distinguished Service Order for gallantry. This in recognition of his conduct during the night of 15/16 September, 1916 when 1st KSLI were heavily engaged at the "Quadrilateral". All attempts to dislodge the enemy from this fiercely held position on the Somme (close to Morval) being in vain and abandoned by midday. In the afternoon the Shropshires came under heavy bombardment from twelve-inch guns - and again throughout the next day. Captain James being mortally wounded during the evening of the 17th and succumbing to his wounds a month later on 15 October.

To the chancel now and here a brass plaque tells how on 13 February, 1920 the organ [built by the Worcester firm of Nicholsen & Co.] was dedicated by the Lord Bishop of Birmingham at St. Peter's. This having been installed as a thank-offering for victory and in memory of those who fell in the Great War.

HIGHNAM - GLOUCESTERSHIRE

Church of the Holy Innocents
Just off the A40 close to Gloucester, Highnam has one of the most beautifully decorated church interiors in the country. Holy Innocents being founded by Thomas Gambier Parry (father of composer Sir Hubert Parry) of Highnam Court - work beginning in 1848 and completed three years later in 1851. By architect Henry Woodyer, the building has exceptional craftsmanship throughout, a feature being its magnificent wall painting - designed and painted by Thomas Gambier Parry himself.

The parish war memorial is indeed worthy of such a fine place. Plain in design, but gleaming with colour, the names, ranks, regiments, place and dates of death of ten men are recorded within a border of blue highlighted with gold. Beginning the list, the names appear by order of death, we have Private Albert Mogg of the 1/5th King's Own Royal Lancaster Regiment - killed 12 March, 1915 in trenches at Wulverghem. This battalion of Territorials had only been in France since the previous 15 February and were still under instruction from regular troops.

Next we have Lance-Corporal Henry Harold Crook, who died in training at Tidworth Camp - you can see his grave in the churchyard (south-east part) - then Private Ernest Skillern. Killed 21 June, 1916 (not on 20th as stated on memorial) just as the 2/5th Gloucesters were being relieved from their trenches at Fauquissart near Laventie.

The remaining men would all lose their lives during 1917. Private Henry Charles Cuff was thirty-one when he died at home on 19 February, 1917 - another Highnam soldier who's grave can be seen in the churchyard (south of church) - then John Butt Ellis - who, with his brother (he was also killed) will be dealt with later.

Proudly displayed on the Commonwealth War Graves Commission headstone of Lance-Corporal Henry Crook, the badge of the Royal Gloucestershire Hussars. Church of the Holy Innocents, Highnam.

Corporal Harry Hyett, another Gloucestershire Regiment soldier fell on 5 April, 1917 as the 1/5th Battalion went into action at Lempire "....the attacking troops, who assaulted the position in fine style" (Wyrall). Private Edward Brain, Queen's Own Royal West Kent Regiment, as the memorial states, died from his wounds in France on 10 May - as did Lance-Corporal Reginald Hatch of the Royal Warwickshire Regiment on 13 October.

Just before his death on 2 December, 1917, Lieutenant William James Pearce's battalion, the 2/5th Gloucesters (not 1/5 as stated on memorial), had moved by train to Royaucourt, then in buses to Fins. Here the men stood by and awaited orders to move forward at a moments notice. The next moved was to Gonnelieu - where the Gloucesters were in close support of attacking troops - then orders came to advance through the village of Villers Plouich and on to a position behind Welsh Ridge. Here a night-flying aircraft dropped a bomb, hitting an

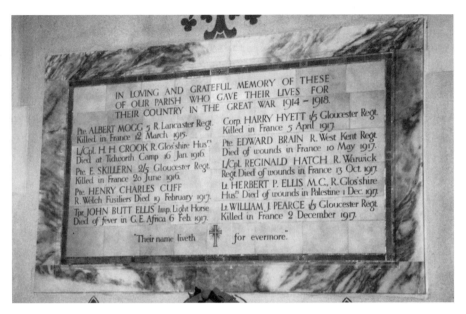

A beautiful war memorial for a beautiful church, Holy Innocents, Highnam.

ammunition dump close to the battalion and causing just under seventy casualties. In the pitch dark, the battalion then advanced onto the ridge itself "....the Commanding Officer [Lieutenant-Colonel G.F. Collett] led the foremost company through the Hindenburg wire; the rest of the battalion followed and the new positions were found.....At dawn the enemy attacked La Vacquerie, driving in the Warwicks and Glosters. That morning Lieut. W.J. Pearce, one of Gloucester's best footballers, was killed" (Barnes).

Moving back into the churchyard, first note the third Commonwealth War Graves Commission headstone located there (those of Henry Crook and Henry Cuff already mentioned) – that of Gunner F.T. Trinder, Royal Garrison Artillery, who died 12 August, 1920. This west of the church.

Also in the churchyard at Holy Innocents is a family headstone that commemorates the deaths on active service of two brothers – Second-Lieutenant Herbert Pearce Ellis and Trooper John Butt Ellis. Serving with the Royal Gloucestershire Hussars Yeomanry, Herbert Ellis (he was awarded the Military Cross) was killed in Palestine. The enemy – who had been making desperate attempts to drive the Yeomen from their positions on high ground north and north-east of Jaffa - on the nights of 29 and 30 November put forward a series of heavy counter-attacks and it would be during the latter assault, at 1 am (1 December), that Herbert was killed "....while his troop was gallantly filing a gap in the 8th A.L.H. [Australian Light Horse] line" (Fox).

Turning now to his elder brother John (aged thirty-seven), we learn from the records held by the Commonwealth War Graves Commission that he was, at the time of war being declared in 1914, resident in South Africa and an employee of Messrs Stewart and Lloyd of Johannesburg. As a trooper with the 2nd South African Horse, he served in East Africa - where he died on 8 January, 1917 - and was buried there at Dodma Cemetery, Tanzania.

KILPECK - HEREFORDSHIRE

St. Mary and St. David

"One of the most perfect Norman village churches in England" (Pevsner), the Romanesque St. Mary and St. David's at Kilpeck (on the A465, nine miles south-west of Hereford) is certainly famous for its outstanding carvings - both in and outside of the building. The whole day, perhaps, can be spent with these, but do take time to look on the north wall of the nave where an illuminated Roll of Honour commemorating the men of the parish that fell in the Great War. Below (in full colour) the flags of the 1914-1918 Allied Nations, the names of five men are recorded - George Jones, Benjamin James Porter, John Pitt, Edwin Powell and Richard Henry Small.

Five men from Kilpeck below the flags of the Allied Nations.

LONGHOPE - GLOUCESTERSHIRE

Longhope's fine lion memorial sits on the main Monmouth road (the A4136 about nine miles west of Gloucester) above the dates "1914-1918". Recently added at the base, a stone tablet recording the names of those lost in both world wars, together with that of one soldier who died in 1973. Further along the road is the turn off for the village - passing through this and on to All Saints.

Longhope's proud lion.

All Saints

Thirteenth century, "but severely restored in 1869 by A.W. Maberly" (Verey), the first war memorial at All Saints will be seen on the north wall of the nave. White marble mounted on black, this commemorates the death in Cairo, on 22 December, 1918, of Major Basil Frank Nell. Mentioned in Despatches and an officer with 519 Field Company, Royal Engineers - part of the 60th (2/2nd London) Division - Basil Nell was buried at Cairo War Memorial Cemetery, three miles south of the city.

On now to the south transept where there are two memorials dedicated to members of the parish. One, in carved oak and showing an angel holding a cross and laurel wreath, includes a list of twenty-two names. These belonging to those that

More flags and emblems at All Saints, Longhope.

died. On the other, an illuminated Roll of Honour, there are one hundred and thirty-three. These the names of those from the parish of Longhope that served in the forces during the war.

To the churchyard now and east of the church a stone Celtic cross commemorates Second-Lieutenant Donald John Stuart Chapman of the 8th Royal Fusiliers. Mortally wounded during the 7 July, 1916 fighting at Ovillers on the Somme - his battalion went into action eight hundred strong at 8.26 am, it numbered just one hundred and sixty by nightfall - Donald Chapman subsequently died at Abbeville on 13 July. Note also the war grave north of the church belonging to Private G.C. Payne of the King's (Shropshire Light Infantry). Eighteen when he died on 13 January, 1821 and the son of George and Helen Payne of Chessgrove, just south of the church.

LYDNEY - GLOUCESTERSHIRE

The West Gloucestershire town of Lydney lies close to the River Severn about nine miles north-east of Chepstow. St. Mary's, its tall spire being clearly visible on the right as you leave the A48, dating from at least the thirteenth century. Opposite the church, and at the entrance to Church Gardens, stands the town war memorial - a tall Bottony cross of local Forest Blue Stone. Carved into three sides of the hexagonal pedestal are the names of those from the area that fell in the Great War. Eighty-two in number, these are accompanied by regiments, but no ranks (save for those of four officers and four non commissioned officers) are given.

Of the eighty-two names, no less than sixty-seven men served in British infantry battalions. Thirty-six of these being in ten different battalions of the Gloucestershire Regiment. Of these, the 7th, 8th and 10th are well represented - almost a quarter of the total men killed serving in one or other of these three Kitchener's "New Army" formations.

In June, 1915, the 7th Gloucesters sailed from Avonmouth for Egypt. The battalion subsequently fighting at Gallipoli and in Mesopotamia. The 8th Battalion, having landed in France on 18 July, 1915, would be in time for the horrific fighting at Loos on 25 September. Action was seen on the Somme, July-November, 1916, Messines and Ypres, 1917 and on the Somme again in 1918. This time during the bloody March battles of St. Quentin and Bapaume.

Also to serve on the Western Front, was the 10th Gloucesters. Arriving in France on 17 August, 1915, this battalion of civilian volunteers was soon attached to the seasoned regulars of the 1st Infantry Division. The fighting at Loos and the Hohenzollern Redoubt followed in October, then the Somme battles of July–September, 1916. In 1917 the battalion was involved in operations on the Flanders Coast, and the defence of Nieuport, before the horrors of the Ypres Salient and Passchendaele. The last year of the war saw action at Estaires, Hazebrouck, Epéhy, the St. Quentin Canal and Beaurevoir Line.

Four men served as Territorials – one in the 4th Battalion, Gloucestershire Regiment, and two in the 2/5th. As the memorial states, Private Albert Freeman was a member of the Royal Gloucestershire Hussars Yeomanry (Headquarters in Gloucester). Sometime in his service, however, he transferred to the 2nd Worcestershire Regiment, with whom he was killed in France on the 2nd November, 1916.

Of those members of the Royal Navy and Royal Marines that lost their lives, the death of George Richard James is notable. He being one of over six hundred killed when his ship, HMS *Vanguard* blew up on 9 July, 1917 while lying in Scapa Flow. He was eighteen years old and the son of George and Francis Annie James of 9 Cookson Terrace, Lydney.

In his history of the 7th North Staffordshire Regiment, L.R. Missen records how that battalion received its baptism of fire immediately after landing at Cape Helles, Gallipoli on 11 July, 1915. The Staffords under shell fire having to quickly dig trenches in the many nullahs and gullies running down to the beach. Having moved up into the firing line, the battalion would sustain its first casualties when the Turks made a desperate attack on 19 July. Over sixty were killed or wounded, among them Captain Clifford George Grail who died from his wounds on the 23rd. Aged twenty-four, Clifford Grail, BA (Hons, Cantab.) went to St. John's College, Cambridge.

The names of three other officers appear on the memorial. Born at Bream, Gloucestershire, Lieutenant Angus John Charles Dodgson was twenty-two when he was killed in action on 10 November, 1917. He had only just joined his battalion, the 2/5th Gloucestershire Regiment, and is noted in their records as having, prior to moving up into the line known as "Chemical Works Sector" – "....entertained large crowds in Arras with his wonderful conjuring tricks." He is buried in Sunken Road Cemetery, Fampoux, France.

Buried in Belgium, Lijssenthoek Military Cemetery, is Captain Sidney Reginald Hockaday of the 2nd Monmouthshire Regiment (headquarters in Pontypool) – the cemetery register of which notes that his parents lived in Sydney, Australia. Captain Hockaday died from his wounds on 2 September, 1916. Captain Hugh Jones, MC is buried in the churchyard at St. Mary's.

St. Mary's

In 1921 a war memorial in the form of a window and lychgate were erected by parishioners at the church. On the gate the inscription in Latin: *"Mementote Fratres Apud Deum Nos Tratium Pro Patria Mortuorum MCMXIV - MCMXVIII"* (Remember Brothers Before God Our Fellow Countrymen Who Died For Their Fatherland 1914–1918). The window of four lights is on the north aisle and has the dedication: "A.O.D.G. and in loving memory of those from this parish who fell in the Great War 1914-1919."

Below the window, and forming its sill, five panels of the same Forest Blue Stone as the memorial, record details of those that died. Names and regiments are again shown, but on this occasion they are ninety-two in number. Three of those inscribed on the memorial do not appear below the window. But there are thirteen additional names.

A "Death Penny" set into a headstone at St. Mary's, Lydney.

At the west end of the church another fine window, featuring the figures of Christ, Zacharias and St. Elizabeth, commemorates the death in France of a local soldier - "Be thou fateful unto death and I will give thee a crown of life. In ever loving memory of Harry Richards No. 13587 8th Gloucesters who fell in action July 23rd 1916 aged 27 years only son of Joseph & Eliza Richards & Grandson of the late Jamesimm, all of Primrose Hill Lydney" - are the words chosen for its dedication. Primrose Hill is on the northern edge of Lydney.

It was at 4 am on 23 July, 1916, that the 8th Gloucesters were relieved from the front line at Bazentine-le-Petit on the Somme. Just prior to that, the battalion had taken part in a failed attack on the German Switch Line cutting through the northern edge of High Wood. The casualties recorded in the battalion war diary are given as two hundred killed, wounded or missing.

There are four war graves within the churchyard. Appearing neither on the town memorial, or that within the church, is the name of Lieutenant F.A.C. Howells who died at home on 24 March, 1920. He had served with the 9th Worcestershire Regiment – which he had joined in Mesopotamia on 25 April, 1917. On 16 November, 1918, the 9th Worcestershire – then stationed in North Persia – sailed for The Caucasus, and there, on 6 December, Lieutenant Howells led an escort from Baku to Batum on the Black Sea. This being to protect the first oil train since the signing of the Armistice.

The war diary of the 13th Gloucestershire Regiment notes that Captain Hugh Jones, MC was wounded in action on 26 March, 1917 and again a year later on 23 March. He died at home on the following 10 November. Private

The grave of Lydney's Harbour Master also remembering a son at St. Mary's.

C. Pinchin, 14th Worcestershire Regiment, died 11 September, 1916, and Private G.H. Saysum, wounded while serving with the 7th Gloucesters, on 26 November, 1919. He was twenty-two.

The churchyard also contains a number of family graves that commemorate servicemen buried overseas. South of the church a headstone records that Jim Lewis, Master Mariner, died on active service on 19 October, 1918 and was buried at Marseilles. This principal French commercial port served throughout the First World War as the Base of Indian troops in France. Many ships of the Royal and Merchant Navies passing through it. The main cemetery at Marseilles is located at Mazargues to the south-east of the town. Here 1st Officer J.S. Lewis of the SS *Singapore*, and the son of one time Harbour Master at Lydney Docks, Samuel Kingscote Lewis, is buried among over one thousand, two hundred other war graves.

East of the church, the Saunders brothers are remembered – Arthur, who died aged twenty-five on 1 November, 1916, and Charles who was twenty-nine when he was killed on 7 September, 1917. Also brothers were Ralph Leslie and George Gerald Frank Fisher, the sons of William and Mary Fisher of Rose Cottage, Primrose Hill, Lydney. Gunner Ralph Fisher served with the 124th Battery, 28th Brigade, Royal Field Artillery and was twenty-six when he died of wounds on 26 April, 1917. He was buried at Barlin Cemetery in France. Interred at Marcoing British Cemetery, France was Private George Fisher who was killed in action when the 4th Worcesters took part in the "First Tank Attack" at Cambrai on 20 November, 1917. He was thirty-four.

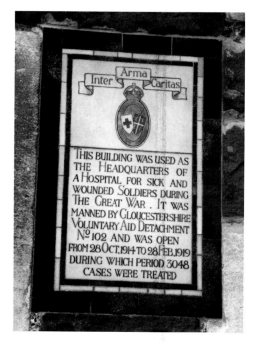

A former use for an old building at Lydney. Plaque by the entrance to the Town Hall.

There are also a number of graves bearing commemoration inscriptions located in part of the churchyard designated as a "Conservation Area". The grave of Elizabeth Eleanor Hyett of 13 Bath Place, Lydney also remembers her husband, Private Albert Henry Hyett who was killed in action on 25 October, 1917 in Macedonia. "His duty done," notes the inscription, Albert Hyett is shown as being buried at Osman Kamilia, Salonika. But his last resting place was the Struma Military Cemetery about forty miles from Salonika, where, after the Armistice the graves from a number of battlefield and churchyard cemeteries were brought in and concentrated.

To the next of kin, large bronze plaques, "Death Pennies", were issued bearing the names of their relatives. Approximately six inches in diameter, that given to Private Harold George Wellington was set into the headstone of his family plot at St. Mary's.

Town Hall

Built by W.H. Seth-Smith in 1888 from land donated by one C. Bathurst Esq., Lydney Town Hall in 1910 comprised a hall, ninety-three feet by forty, with a raised stage, dressing and cloak rooms (*Kelly's Directory of Gloucestershire*). Today this fine building at the junction of Church Road and High Street features a modern clock above its doorway. Blue-faced and presented by the local Royal British Legion in memory of members passed. Of First World War interest, however, is the colourful tablet set just to the right of the doorway. This commemorating the period - October, 1914 to February, 1919 - when the building was used by the Gloucestershire VAD.

MADLEY - HEREFORDSHIRE

Church of the Nativity of the Blessed Virgin Mary

Set in the wide valley of the River Wye, Madley lies on the B4352 about six miles west of Hereford. There was a church here as early as 550 AD - but the present building is somewhat later. The main north porch being Norman and part of a stone church built around 1050-1100.

On the south side of the spacious St. Mary's is the Chilstone Chapel. Began in c1330, here we find - "In gratitude and honour to brave men" - the parish war memorial. A finely-carved and highly-decorated oak panel listing on two sides fifty-nine names - these below the heading "These served their king and country in the war of 1914-1919." Then, in the centre, under "These made the supreme sacrifice", another nine: F. Bagley - S. Bethel - G. Cook -

Those that were killed and those that served remembered at the Church of the Nativity of the Blessed Virgin Mary, Madley.

G. Dyke - S. Hancocks - W. Jones - W.J. Jones - C.V. Mayo and A. Williams. Note both the Arms of the Bishopric of Hereford (left) and to the right the Arms of the City itself (three lions within a border of ten silver saltires). Close by, and as a thanks offering for victory, the organ was given by the parishioners of Madley.

MINSTERWORTH - GLOUCESTERSHIRE

St. Peter's

Always susceptible to flooding, the old medieval church at Minsterworth - on the bank of the River Severn approximately four miles west of Gloucester - was demolished in 1869. The present church by Henry Woodyer being opened in the following year and built on foundations set four feet above those of the old building. Just inside the churchyard a tall stone cross forms the parish war memorial. Its eight-sided base having a series of bronze plaques attached and bearing the names of those that were killed. Erected by parishioners - these seem to be recent additions and possibly replacing original, and now worn, lettering. There are nine names, these, and the dedication, being highlighted in white paint.

Inside the church at its west end, we find two handwritten Rolls of Honour. One listing those that served, the other the nine that fell. Move now to the south side of the nave and here a beaten-copper plaque bearing the badge of the East Lancashire Regiment commemorates the death in Mesopotamia of a young officer - the son of Charles Bartlett - vicar of St. Peter's, 1906 to 1930. In raised letters the dedication reads: "To the glory of God and in loving memory of Robert Nigel Oldfield Bartlett, captain, East Lancashire Regiment, mortally wounded at Felahiyeh in Mesopotamia on April 5th 1916 while leading his company in the victorious night attack of the 13th 'Iron' Division on the Turkish trenches. He died April 6th 1916, age 22. Younger son of the Revd. Charles Oldfield Bartlett, M.A. vicar of this parish and Edith his wife." The wording ends with the words "He that loseth his life for my sake shall find it."

The "Iron" Division, the 13th (Western) Division, was formed at the beginning of the war and included Robert Bartlett's battalion - the 6th East Lancashire Regiment. He left with them for Gallipoli in June, 1915, and while in action at Sari Bair (8-10 August) was wounded. The East Lancashire left Gallipoli in the following December, and via Mudros and Egypt, joined the Mesopotamia Expeditionary Force near Basra in February, 1916. The 13th Division now to assist in yet another attempt to relieve General Townsend's troops besieged at Kut. By 2

April, the 6th East Lancashire had taken over support trenches in readiness for an attack on the Turkish positions at Hanna. The British went forward at 4.53 am – clearing all before them – but it would not be until late in the evening that the East Lancashire would have its chance. Following the line of advance, the battalion later overran and cleared the enemy from Suwaikiya March on the left of the Turkish line. Casualties totalling ten officers and one hundred and eighty other ranks. Mortally wounded, Captain Bartlett was later buried in the Amara War Cemetery on the left bank of the Tigris.

Minsterworth's war dead remembered in the churchyard of St. Peter's.

Among others commemorated at St. Peter's are Private Howard Selwyn of the Auckland Regiment, New Zealand Forces. Wounded at Gallipoli and subsequently dying at sea on 10 August, 1915 while being evacuated to hospital. His father, William Selwyn, was a local sheep dealer. Sergeant Claude Macey served with the 2nd Welsh Regiment and was one of the two hundred and eight casualties incurred by that battalion as it attacked High Wood on the Somme – 8 September, 1916.

Just over a year later the first of the Mayo brothers would be killed. Twenty-two year old Private Cyril George Mayo of the 2/4th Gloucestershire Regiment being one of those that fell during operations near Cambrai on 3 December, 1917. "At about 8.15" – notes a report written by the Commanding Officer of 2/4th Battalion, Lieutenant-Colonel D.G. Barnsley – "the enemy put down a very heavy barrage on the whole of the frontage held by this battalion and attacked in very large numbers." Cyril's elder brother, Leonard Frank, was killed on 27 May, 1918 as his battalion (1st Worcestershire) fought north of the River Aisne. Records note that the brothers' parents, George and Jane Mayo, lived at Church House, Minsterworth. Jane being shown in the 1910 edition of *Kelly's Directory of Gloucestershire* as a shopkeeper.

Captain Eric Howard Harvey received his first Commission in October, 1915 and just under a year later joined the 1/5th Gloucestershire Regiment (7 August. 1916) at Cramont, France. He was posted to "B" Company, notes the battalion war diary, which, on 10 September, 1916 also records the award of his Military Cross. This in recognition of his conduct during the fighting on the Somme (Ovillers sector) the previous month. At sometime transferred, Eric Harvey joined the 2/5th Gloucestershire (this the second-line of the Gloucester-based 5th Territorial Battalion) at St. Venant on 20 April, 1918. He was put in charge of "C" Company, and on 29 April was wounded while his men were out digging new trenches close to Robequ.

Soon back on duty, Captain Harvey was in the forward area again when on 29 September the 2/5th Gloucestershire took over trenches in front of Estaires. The battalion was to take part in an attack next day - "C" Company to lead the assault on a strongly held enemy position known as "Junction Post". "Fighting went on at close quarters but 'Junction Post was occupied...'" (war diary). One of two officers killed on 30 September, Eric Harvey was subsequently buried in Estaires Communal Cemetery. The service (records A.F. Barnes in his history of the 2/5th Gloucestershire) being attended by men from "A" Company, still thick with mud from the forward trenches. "His death", wrote one officer, "was a loss the battalion could ill afford. The best of company commanders and the cheeriest of comrades, he displayed the utmost gallantry on every occasion. His disregard of danger inspired his men, who would go anywhere under his command. He was killed by a machine gun bullet while walking back to his Company Headquarters from the front line." For his gallantry on 30 September, Captain Eric Harvey was awarded a Bar to his Military Cross. *Note*: Eric Harvey was the brother of Frederick William ("Will") Harvey - poet and friend of Ivor Gurney.

MITCHELDEAN - GLOUCESTERSHIRE

St. Michael and All Angels
On the northern edge of the Forest of Dean, Mitcheldean off the A4136 lies some eleven miles from Gloucester. The spacious St. Michael and All Angels, it has three aisles, in part dates from the thirteenth century - but most of the structure in fourteenth and fifteenth. Look first at the short white cross as you enter the churchyard from the High Street. Erected by the Mitcheldean and Abenhall British Legion to commemorate the dead of both world wars, this has a separate

tablet bearing a metal plate inscribed with the names of those killed from both areas. For 1914-1918 - twenty-nine for Mitcheldean and ten for Abenhall just to the south-east.

But an earlier memorial to those that fell in the First World War will be found inside the church and in the form of a fine oak pulpit. Just the Mitcheldean names (twenty-two this time) are carved into the back panel leading up to the canopy, the dedication - "To the glory of God and in grateful memory of the men from this parish who laid down their lives in the Great War 1914-19" - appearing around the base. The same twenty-two names appear again at the west end of the church - neatly hand-painted as part of a Roll of Honour. Note the heading - "European War 1914-15" - which possible suggest that the work was carried out before the end of hostilities in 1918.

A fine oak pulpit to remember the dead of Mitcheldean. St. Michael and All Angels Church.

Return to the churchyard now, and here in the west corner is the grave of Private William George Millin. He served with the 11th Bedfordshire Regiment and died on 18 November, 1918.

MUCH DEWCHURCH - HEREFORDSHIRE

St. David's

Lying below low wooded hills south of Hereford, Much Dewchurch has been a Christian parish since Roman times. Its name being a corruption of an earlier version - Llandewi (Church of St. David). The village is situated on the Ross to Hay-on-Wye road (B4348) about six miles south-west of Hereford. Its church being mostly Norman and comprising nave and chancel. Enter St. David's by its timber

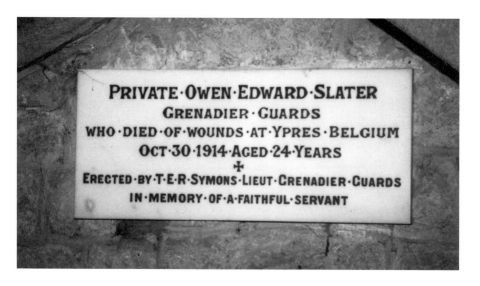

An officer remembers his servant at St. David's, Much Dewchurch.

south porch. Fourteenth century and for many years welcoming members of the Symonds family - in 1914 Captain Thomas Raymond Symonds being Lord of the Manor and resident at The Mynde. A Tudor house just south-west of the village.

Among many monuments to the family, we see in the church a small white-marble tablet set into a recess on the south side. This mentioning Lieutenant Thomas Edward Raymond Symonds - son of Captain Symonds and an officer of the Grenadier Guards who fought with the 1st Battalion during the First World War. But he was not killed. The memorial being erected by him as a commemoration to his servant - Private Owen Edward Slater.

Born at Cheadle in Staffordshire, Owen Slater landed in Belgium with his officer on 7 October, 1914. The 1st Grenadier Guards having arrived at Southampton two days before and crossing in two vessels - the SS *Armenian* and SS *Turcoman*. The latter, recalled the Rt. Hon. Sir Frederick Ponsonby in his war history of the Grenadier Guards, being "....just a cattle-boat." Two train journeys later the Grenadiers were at Ghent on 9 October, where, from a local dye-works, the Belgian authorities issued large rolls of velvet in lieu of blankets.

The enemy (parties of Uhlans) were first sighted on 14 October just outside Ypres - but it would be five days later, and further forward at Kruiseecke, that the Grenadiers went into action for the first time. For the next ten days the battalion would be under constant fire - almost half its strength being lost as the enemy pushed its way forward. German shells would also account for a great number of deaths and casualties - some sixty-per-minute being calculated as landing on part of the Grenadiers' line during 26 October alone. Buried alive, many had to be rescued from under as much as three foot of earth. Fatally wounded sometime during this period, Owen Slater would die on 30 October. He has no know grave and is remembered on the Menin Gate Memorial to the missing at Ypres. He was twenty-four.

Also to lose his life during the early weeks of the war, and commemorated at St. David's (brass plaque, south wall of nave), was Captain Harold Lutwyche Helme of the 1st Loyal North Lancashire Regiment. The only son of Harold and Mary Helme (King's Thorn, west of the village), Captain Helme was born on 3 August, 1878 (baptised at St. David's on 15 September) and having been educated at Haileybury College obtained his commission in 1899. He subsequently served in the Boer War of 1899-1902, in which he was wounded, and later in West Africa took part in the Onitsha Hinterland and Bende-Onitsha and Hinterland Expeditions.

Leaving Tournay Barracks, Aldershot on 12 August, 1914, the 1st Loyal North Lancashire sailed on the SS *Agapenor* from Southampton next day - the battalion then moving forward from Havre via train and road and reaching Givry on 23 August. The British Expeditionary Force was now in retreat, and falling back the battalion would arrive at Bernay on 5 September. But it was now time to advance and moving forward again, the Marne was crossed at Nogent on 9 September, followed by the Aisne at Bourg four days later. Next day, 14 September and date of Harold Helme's death, the Loyals went into action at Troyon - where heavy fighting was going on at a factory. "The position was reached", notes the battalion records, "the factory was carried and held; but the enemy was in great strength and counter-attacked heavily...." With ammunition beginning to run out, the Loyals were forced to withdraw. Their casualties numbering some fourteen officers and more than five hundred other ranks.

Captain Harold Lutwyche Helme's name also appears on the La Ferte-Sous-Jouarre Memorial. A monument close to the South (or left) bank of the Marne commemorating those with no known graves who fell in action during the Retreat from Mons and subsequent advance to the Aisne.

To the churchyard now where buried therein is twenty-one-year-old Private Albert Ivor Stanley Probert of the 1st Herefordshire Regiment. The only son of Albert and Martha Elizabeth Probert, who died on 17 February, 1917. Albert

Probert is one of seven names appearing on a tall stone cross close to the church. Erected by parishioners and found to the side of the road as you leave the village heading north-west.

NEWNHAM-ON-SEVERN - GLOUCESTERSHIRE

Approximately eleven miles south-west of Gloucester, on the western bank of the River Severn, lies Newnham. Its tall war memorial situated on the side of the road and looking down on the busy traffic as it passes through the village on the A48. The base of the cross numbers eight sides, one of which bears the dedication in raised metal letters: "In honoured memory of the men of Newnham who fell in the Great War 1914-1918."

On the remaining seven sides the names and ranks of those who fell: Sub-Lieutenant Geoffrey Armitage, Second-Lieutenant F. Batty Atkinson, Second-Lieutenant W. Bingham Barling, Corporal Stephen Brobyn, Gunner John Burton, Sapper H. George Caudle, Private Frederick C. Cooper, Private Alfred F. Cummins, Private Frank French, Private Ralph Drew, Lieutenant Roy M. Hadingham, Private John R. Hall, Private Herbert W. Hatton, Private Albert W. Hooper, Lieutenant William J. Kerr, Lance-Corporal Frank King, Second-Lieutenant E. Archibald C. McLanghlin, Lieutenant H. Guy B. McLanghlin, Gunner Sydney Ryder, Private Albert Stephens, Captain Clive W. Taunton and Private Frank Wellington. Note how the names are set out in strict alphabetical order regardless of rank, and how those for the Second World War, together with a soldier killed in Kenya, 1954, have been added below.

Born in Knaresborough, Yorkshire, Frederick Atkinson was just nineteen when he was killed in France on 25 September, 1918. He served with the 87th Brigade, Royal Field Artillery which, as part of the 19th (Western) Division, had recently seen action during the Battle of the Aisne. Sapper Herbert George Caudle's unit, the 82nd Field Company, Royal Engineers, was also part of the 19th Division and at time of his death, 18 November, 1916, was in support of the infantry as it fought the last hours of the Battle of the Ancre. From No. 2 Severn Street, Newnham, twenty-five year old Herbert Caudle is buried at Connaught Cemetery on the Somme.

Also to fall during the Somme fighting of 1916 - on 20 July - was Private Herbert Hatton of the 10th Gloucestershire Regiment. This battalion having arrived in the area on 5 July and after moving forward to the support line at

Fricourt undertook its first duty - the burial of some four to five hundred bodies from the recent fighting. The Gloucesters moved into Shelter Wood on 19 July and while there worked on the digging of a new front line at Bazentine-le-Petit Wood. Herbert Hatton has no known grave and is commemorated on the Thiepval Memorial to the missing.

We turn now to two young officers of the 7th Seaforth Highlanders - the sons of Vivian Guy and Edith McLaughlin of Brightlands, Newnham. It would be on 29 September, 1915 that the 9th (Scottish) Division, this including 7th Seaforth, was ordered to move north to the Ypres Salient. The men having had barely time to scrape off the mud and slime from their recent experiences at the Battle of Loos. Trenches were taken over near Hill 60 on 5 October and here, on 9 November, the first of the brothers was killed. Edward McLaughlin was the battalion Machine Gun Officer and having gone over to attend one of his guns a shell exploded killing him instantly. His Commanding Officer wrote: "He went up to the trenches to have a look round his machine guns, and at 3.15 pm was talking to his gun team at the gun emplacement when a shell landed on the exact spot and killed the poor boy." Twenty year old Edward was buried at Railway Dugouts Cemetery (Transport Farm), Zillebeke.

Two years his junior, his brother Hubert would take part in the 12 October, 1916 attack on Snag Trench, close to Eaucourt-l'-Abbaye on the Somme, and number among those killed or mortally wounded as heavy machine gun fire tore through the ranks of the 7th Seaforth as they left their trenches and stepped into no man's land. The British barrage was also falling short and contributed to the four hundred and sixty-seven casualties from the battalion since it went forward on 10 October. Joining the Army in April, 1915, Hubert went out to France on 18 July, 1916 and having died from his wounds was buried in Warlencourt British Cemetery.

Another officer to lose his life on the Somme in 1916 was twenty-one-year-old Captain Clive Warneford Taunton of the 2nd Monmouthshire Regiment. One of the original officers that went out with the battalion in November, 1914. The 1916 Battle of the Somme officially over as from 18 November, the Monmouths were, while in their camp at Montauban, under occasional bombardment from the enemy's guns. A direct hit on Captain Taunton's tent killing him instantly on 25 November. The son of Colonel I.E.D. Taunton of the Red House, Newnham, Clive was buried in Bernafay Wood British Cemetery close to where he was killed.

Also from the Monmouthshire, this time the Abergavenny-based 3rd Battalion, was Private Albert William Hooper. Twenty-one when he died at

Frezenberg Ridge on 5 May, 1915. With no known grave, Albert Hooper's name appears on the Menin Gate Memorial to the missing.

Seven of the twenty-two men on the Newnham memorial are commemorated at St. Peter's Church south of the village.

St. Peter's

St. Peter's is on a promontory overlooking the river, across the Vale of Berkeley and on to the Cotswolds. The earliest records of a church at Newnham are dated 1018, which, notes a guide to St. Peter's prepared by the Newnham History Research Group, was the first of probably six to occupy the site. One building was badly damaged during the Civil War, and in 1874 another, being in such a bad state of repair, was demolished. St. Peter's was soon rebuilt, but tragedy stuck in 1881 when a fire almost completely destroyed the church. In its replacement (the present church) stone fragments from a c1230 building can be traced in the fabric.

On the wall of the south aisle, and below a Royal British Legion Standard, two hand-written Rolls of Honour commemorate those that fell in two world wars. Simple lists of names, and with no dedication, the frame to the left records below the dates 1914-1918, twenty-two names in two columns. Those shown on the village memorial.

Three of those listed on the St. Peter's Roll have individual memorials within the church. At the end of the south aisle, the Lady Chapel - dedicated to Our Lady, and Saints Catherine, Margaret and Mary Magdalene - includes to the right of the alter, a memorial window to four members of the Kerr Family. Dr. William Charles Kerr, notes the Church Guide, was left property in Newnham ("The Haie") by his cousin, Lady Davy. Widow of Sir Humphrey Davy - inventor of the miners' safety lamp. Installed in 1946, the window is illustrated by naval and military devices, and provides a fine record of military service - the first member of the family, William Kerr, dying from wounds received in the Crimea, and two others, Royal Navy and Royal Artillery officers, falling during the Second World War.

Shown above the badge of the East Lancashire Regiment is the Mullet and Stringed Bugle-horn of the Cameronians (Scottish Rifles). Born in 1890, Lieutenant William John Kerr was a regular soldier with that regiment. Leaving the Royal Military College, Sandhurst in September, 1909, he travelled with the 2nd Cameronians to Malta two years later in September, 1911. Here the battalion remained until it sailed for England on 15 September, 1914. The Cameronians spent a few weeks in camp at Hursley Park near Winchester, then having received orders to move overseas, landed in France on 5 November. The battalion had reached La

Flinque by 18 November, and on the 21st took over trenches in the Chapigny sector. Here, on 1 February, 1915, records the battalion war diary, one man was killed, and another, Lieutenant W.J. Kerr, wounded. Having returned home, William John Kerr succumbed to his wounds and subsequently died on 10 March, 1915. The day that over four hundred and fifty of his battalion would become casualties at Neuve Chapell back in France. He was buried in a family plot overlooking the Severn in the churchyard at St. Peter's.

At the west end of the church, and above a memorial to his father, a brass cross, decorated with a floral design, commemorates the death of a young trainee pilot. On a plaque below the inscription:"To the glory of God and in memory of Prob. Flight Sub-Lt. Geoffrey Allen Armitage R.N. late of the Merchant Service. Killed while flying on duty at Hendon

St. George helps keep the memory alive, at St. Peter's, Newnham-on-Severn, of twenty-three-year-old Second-Lieutenant William Bingham Barling.

Dec. 11. 1915. Age 22. Blessed are the pure in heart." The son of Henry and Katharine Armitage of The Nab, Newnham, Geoffrey Armitage served with the Royal Naval Air Service and was killed in an accident at the Hendon Naval Air Station near London. He is also buried in St. Peter's churchyard.

Also at the west end of St. Peters is a fine memorial in coloured mosaic commemorating the only son of William Barling. Below the figure of St. George, the dedication appears on a scroll:"To the glory of God and in memory of William Bingham Barling aged 23 2nd Lieut. 6th Batt. Worcester Regt. who fell in action in Flanders 12 Mar. 1915." Following this, the words "When I Fall I Shall Arise."

Born 8 July, 1892, William Bingham Barling was educated first, at the Priory Preparatory School in Malvern, then from Dean Close, Cheltenham attended Wye College where he was elected to a fellowship of the Surveyors' Institute. He later joined the Inland Revenue office at Gloucester, where he worked in the Valuation Department. When war broke out he immediately enlisted as a private in the 5th Gloucestershire Regiment, but in the following December was gazetted as Second-Lieutenant (on probation), 6th (Reserve) Battalion, Worcestershire Regiment.

Posted to the 3rd Worcesters, then in the Locre area and holding trenches facing the Messines Ridge, William Barling went overseas in February, 1915. The battalion had just survived a severe winter and while in the forward area occupied trenches deep in mud, water and slime.

From 4 to 11 March the Worcesters had been in billets at Locre, but on the 12th would lead a tragic attack on the enemy's line at Spanbroek Hill. In their shallow and flooded assembly trenches, the battalion crouched all morning – visibility was poor, notes one observer, but as the mist cleared the enemy's fire became more accurate.

A glorious family window illustrating years of glorious service. St. Peter's, Newnham-on-Severn.

At 4.10 pm, two companies rose to their feet, and under a hail of bullets went forward. The advance was knee-deep in mud – officers and men falling at every step – but a small party managed to enter, and held, part of the German line for a while. But most of the 3rd Worcesters lay killed or wounded in the mud – total casualties amounting to forty-seven killed, ninety-nine wounded, thirty-two missing. Among the missing, he was last seen at the head of his men, Second-Lieutenant Barling has no known grave.

In addition to the war graves of Geoffrey Armitage and William Kerr, the churchyard contains four family plots giving reference to relatives lost overseas.

North of the church, a family headstone also commemorates the death as a prisoner of war in Germany on 23 May, 1918, of Frederick Charles Cooper. Private Cooper was nineteen when he died and had served with the 1st East Lancashire Regiment. Close by a stone cross records that Lance-Corporal Thomas Francis King of the 2nd Lincolnshire Regiment, also nineteen, having been killed in action on 5 March, 1917, was interred at Bray Military Cemetery in France. Private Albert George Stephens, notes his family's headstone, died of wounds in France in March, 1918. He was thirty-seven and a member of the Royal Army Medical Corps.

North-east of the church is a Hadingham family plot. This recording the fact that twenty-one year old Lieutenant Roy Matthew Hadingham of the 2/4th Gloucestershire Regiment was killed in action at Laventie, France on 26 June, 1916. Having arrived in France a month earlier, the 2/4th Gloucesters had taken over trenches for the first time ("Moated Grange") on 15 June.

NORTHWICK - GLOUCESTERSHIRE

St. Thomas's
The A403 begins close to the old Severn Road Bridge at Junction 1 on the M48 and then runs south, with the river in view, towards Avonmouth. Soon the Northwick turn-off appears and having turned left onto the B4055 you have just a short drive down to the site of St. Thomas's. The main body of the building having been demolished, the west tower of the church being all that remains. Entering the churchyard, and shaded by a small tree, there appears, what at first sight looks like the Gothic-style headstone of a grave. A closer look, however, reveals that the monument is in fact a memorial to two First World War soldiers - Francis Henry Ball and Alfred Job Ball. Both losing their lives at twenty-three-years-old.

Carved into the upper portion of the stonework a double star-design heads several items of military significance - a rifle, entwined with laurel leaves and ammunition bandoliers, with in the centre a service-dress cap. The latter bearing the regimental badge of one of the soldiers commemorated - that of the Royal Gloucestershire Hussars Yeomanry.

Having spent the early months of 1915 on coastal patrol in the King's Lynn, Norfolk area, the Royal Gloucestershire Hussars (RGH) entrained at Hunstanton for Avonmouth on 10 April - ironically, Shoeing Smith Francis Henry Ball now finding himself within a few miles of his home. As part of the 1st South Midland Mounted Brigade, 2nd Mounted Division, the regiment left on the *Minneapollis* and *Saturnia* next day, and having called at Malta, 21 April, arrived at Alexandria on the 24th. The RGH moved into Chatby Camp, close to the city, and from there occupied its time providing various Guards – on one occasion forming an escort to the 1st Sultan of Egypt when he entered Alexandria for the first time.

Orders sending the RGH to Gallipoli were received on 11 August. These stating that the regiment was to leave its horses in Egypt, and in an infantry role, proceeded to the Peninsular with immediate effect. On 14 August, fifteen officers and three hundred and forty-six other ranks left Alexandria on two ships, the *Haverford* and *Ascania*. These taking the Yeomen, first to the Island of Mudros. Later, having transferred to the *Queen Victoria* – a paddle steamer formally on the Isle of Man service – the men were then landed at "A" Beach, Suvla Bay, midnight on 17 August.

The west tower, all that remains of St. Thomas's, Northwick, looks down onto a memorial commemorating the deaths of two members of the Bell family.

The 2nd Mounted Division concentrated in the rear of Lala Baba during the night of 20 August. Here the Yeomanry were to await an advance by the infantry, then to follow on as far as Chocolate Hill. The RGH were now on the eve of their first experiences of active operations. This to take place after mid-day 21 August, the date of Francis Ball's death. "All ranks," records Brigadier-General C.F. Aspinall-Oglander in his history of the Gallipoli campaign (part of the *Official History* series), "were cheerfully excited that afternoon as they sat on the beach behind Lala Baba, watching the warships shooting, and waiting for the order to move."

Soon after 3.30 pm the men of the RGH went forward and upon reaching the open-plain south of the Salt Lake – together with several thousand others – offered an inviting target to the Turkish artillery. Fortunately, notes several records of the operations that afternoon, there were few casualties among the Mounted

Division as a whole - the enemy's shrapnel bursting as it did, too high to cause great damage. The hill was reached by 5 pm, General Aspinall-Oglander recording how the entire Mounted Division had advanced steadily and as if on parade - only moving at the double when ordered to do so.

The next move forward - this coming after less than an hour's rest at Chocolate Hill, and through thick mist and scrub fires - would be in the direction of lines occupied by the 29th Division. But with daylight almost gone there would be no opportunity to attack the enemy and by nightfall the RGH, having been under fire for the first time, dug in about three hundred yards in rear of the 29th Division's lines. Casualties during the advance had amounted to one officer and eleven other ranks killed, four officers and forty-four other ranks wounded. One man was posted as missing. In his records of the RGH, Frank Fox records that Francis Ball's probable burial place was one thousand yards east of Chocolate Hill. Green Hill Cemetery, notes the Commonwealth War Graves Commission, was made after the Armistice by the collection of isolated graves and here Francis Ball is recorded as one of those believed to be occupying an unnamed grave.

The advance of the Yeomanry on 21 August, 1915 is on record as being a great example of courage and disciple. The men being, as they were, "unseasoned Territorials" experiencing their first time under fire. The following is taken from a despatch by General, Sir Ian Hamilton, Commander-in-Chief, Gallipoli: "The advance of these English yeoman was a sight calculated to send a thrill of pride through anyone with a drop of English blood running in their veins. Such superb martial spectacles are rare in modern war."

Alfred Job Ball's relationship to Francis is not known. Brothers possibly, Alfred sharing, as he does, the name Job with the latter's father. He would be approximately three years younger. Being the same age as Francis when he fell in France on 14 June, 1918. Little is known of his military service, save that he was serving with the 8th Gloucestershire Regiment when he died. With no regimental history to consult, we can, however, turn to the battalion war diary to establish where the 8th Gloucesters were on and around the time of death. From this we learn that the battalion, having fought its way through the April, 1918 Battles of Messines, Bailleul and Kemmel, arrived at Chambrecy, 4.30 am, 29 May. Latter, at 9 am, the Gloucesters were sent forward three miles to occupy a line of road running from Lhery to Tramery. Here the battalion came under fire from field guns.

At 8am on 30 May, just after rations, which had to be sent back, arrived, the enemy made a determined attack to the left. This forcing an eventual withdrawal back to Chambrecy. The village itself was attacked on 1 June, the Commanding

Officer, Lieutenant-Colonel R.B. Umfreville noting in the war diary that two of his companies "found themselves enveloped" and all officers of "A" Company had become casualties. The Gloucesters that day losing over two hundred and fifty killed or wounded.

The battalion was moved on 9 June, first to Brigade Reserve at Bois-de-Courton, then next day deeper into the wood and Divisional Reserve. Here the Gloucesters remained until 18 June. Private Ball dying on the 14th. He was buried at Marfaux British Cemetery which lies just south-east of the village on the north-east side of the road to Nanteuil-la-Fosse and on the south-east side of the cross road from Bois-de-Courton to Cuitron.

PETERCHURCH - HEREFORDSHIRE

St. Peter's

In the heart of the Golden Valley, Peterchurch lies on the B4348 twelve miles west of Hereford. The tall one hundred and eighty-six foot spire of its church being seen long before you enter the village. But this spectacular landmark is somewhat younger than the Norman St. Peter's of 1130. Constructed as it was from fibreglass and erected in 1972 to replace the original 1320 spire that, having fell into disrepair, was taken down in 1949.

Buried in St. Peter's churchyard was Private Thomas Sydney Parry of "D" Training Battalion, Machine Gun Corps. Eighteen when he died on 31 October, 1918, his name can also be found on the parish war memorial on the north side of St. Peter's. A tall stone cross bearing at its base the details of six other men: Albert Joseph Hughes - William John Mapp - Moses Metcalf - John Pitt - Thomas Preece and George Walter Verrill.

Before leaving the churchyard visit the grave of Robert Jones (down path from memorial on right). Awarded the Victoria Cross for his part in the Battle of Rorkes Drift - Zulu War of 1879. A bonus perhaps, as is the United States Army Second World War ambulance on view at the garage opposite the churchyard.

St. Peter's itself has no First World War memorials within the church. But do take time to look at the print situated on the south wall directly ahead as you enter. This from Charles Dixon's fine painting showing the Herefordshire Regiment as it advanced towards Azmak Dere under shell-fire - Gallipoli, 8 August, 1915.

PETERSTOW - HEREFORDSHIRE

About two miles west of Ross, Peterstow is reached by turning off the A40 then onto the A49. Pass the Bridstow parish memorial on the right, then after a short distance that for Peterstow appears on a green to the left. On the shaft of a tall stone cross the names of seven men that fought "For God King and Country" are recorded - William Hall, Arthur W. Llewellyn, Henry Miles, David R. Matthews, John F.L. Woodall, Charles Ryder and Thomas Ryder.

Note the Ryder brothers. Charles who was twenty-seven when he died on 6 November, 1917, while serving with the 1/1st Herefordshire Regiment in Palestine and Thomas, a member of the 1st King's Shropshire Light Infantry who fell in France eight months earlier on 10 March, 1917. He was twenty.

No First World War memorials were found at Peterstow church. Completely restored in 1866 - but still including traces of the original Norman building - St. Peter's with its notable spire will be found just along from the memorial and down the lane to the right.

PILNING - GLOUCESTERSHIRE

Pilning lies off the Avonmouth road (A403) close to the River Severn and south of the M4 Motorway. The village war memorial being situated across from the Cross Hands pub and bearing the names on three sides of the those that served, together with the dead from both world wars. Before leaving Pilning take time perhaps, to visit the grave of one of those that died. Private Sydney Pullin of the Machine Gun Corps being buried close by at St. Peter's churchyard.

The dead of two world wars remembered at Pilning.

PODSMEAD - GLOUCESTERSHIRE

Crypt School

Founded in 1539 by John and Joan Cooke at Gloucester's St. Mary de Crypt Church, Southgate Street, the school is now located at Podsmead close to the A38 on the southern outskirts of the city. The war memorial to fifty-eight Old Cryptians killed in the Great War - originally at the school's premises in Friar's Orchard - is now located in the entrance hall at Podsmead. In plain brass, mounted on black marble, the plaque is surmounted by the School Arms in oxidised silver and enamel and was made by Messrs. Marshal & Co. of Cheltenham from a design prepared by one of the school's masters - A.F. Watts, BA, MBE. The unveiling was carried out by Lieutenant-Colonel J.H. Collett, DSO, CMG (commanded the 5th Gloucesters during the war) and dedicated by the Ven. Archdeacon of Norfolk, the Rev. A.R. Buckland - both former pupils.

The contribution made by Old Boys in 1914-1918 is covered in Charles Lepper's comprehensive history of the Crypt School (Alan Sutton, Gloucester, 1989) and he provides the following details: "A total of 329 Old Boys served in the war, of whom 47 won Honours and 22 were Mentioned in Despatches; 97 were Commissioned Officers.....War Honours included five D.S.O.s, three O.B.E.s, sixteen M.C.s (five with Bar), one D.F.C., and one Croix de Guerre."

ROSS-ON-WYE - HEREFORDSHIRE

St. Mary's

The centre of Christian worship at Ross for more than seven hundred years, St. Mary's tall spire soars high above the town. An impressive site from a number of views, but none more so than that from across the river as you come in off the A40 and along the B4260. Cross the spacious nave, through the south aisle and into the sixteenth-century Marke Chapel where the town's war dead are commemorated. See their regimental badges carved on both sides of the screen as you enter. Together with the screen, the fine memorial on the chapel wall was erected in 1920 and in four panels records the names and regiments of ninety-eight men that lost their lives.

Look now to the left of the memorial and here on another tablet we learn that the chapel's altar-rail was given to the church by the wife of a local doctor "In loving remembrance of his self-sacrifice and devotion to duty during the Great War...." Today, little is known of James Ashford Potts, MB, CM, MRCS who died

Regimental badges carved into a memorial screen at St. Mary's, Ross.

14 March, 1919. "Of Palace Pound" notes his memorial, surgeon of St. Mary's Street says *Kelly's Directory* (1913 edition).

Another grateful member of St. Mary's congregation was Mrs Edith Purchas who, according to the church guide, had the organ installed at St. Mary's in 1921 – "She died soon after its dedication and hers was the first funeral at which the instrument was played." A small metal plate attached to the organ tells how Mrs Purchas lived at Chasedale, Ross and how her donation was as a "thanks offering" after the war.

In memory of those from the Ross district that were killed in the First World War, a stone memorial cross was erected in the gardens to the west of St. Mary's. The names appear all around its four-sided base – those for the Second World War, together with one belonging to a soldier killed in the South Atlantic 1982, have now been added.

The Commonwealth War Graves Commission list six war graves at St. Mary's. Before leaving the churchyard look for Sergeant R. Cox of the 1st Herefordshire

Ninety-eight men that lost their lives and a local doctor remembered at St. Mary's, Ross.

Regiment; Private J. Dix, 29th Middlesex Regiment; Private T. Green, an old soldier of fifty-seven that served at home with the Royal Defence Corps; Petty Officer Arthur Kyte of HMS *Vernon*, he was fifty-two; Private C. Ross of the King's Shropshires and Private C.A.M. Smith, another Herefordshire Regiment man.

RUARDEAN - GLOUCESTERSHIRE

St. John's

On a hilltop close to the border with Herefordshire, Ruardean - a few miles west of Cinderford - looks across to the Forest of Dean and the Wye valley. The tall spire of its c1110 church being seen from miles around as you approach the village. The war memorial at St. John's - it was presented to the parish council by Ivor William Baldwin JP - can be found in the south aisle flanked by Royal British Legion Standards and surmounted by a fine representation of the Royal Arms. In bronze

- note how it has been fashioned to look as though a laurel wreath lies between it and the brown and white marble - an oblong tablet records the names (highlighted in gold) of twelve men that were killed.

The first name shown is that of thirty-one-year-old Lieutenant-Commander Ralph Ryall Clayton who was killed at the Battle of Jutland on 31 May, 1916. With a complement of over twelve hundred officers and men, his ship, HMS *Queen Mary,* was lost in the early stages of the fight after several twelve-inch shells from the German battle-cruiser *Derfflinger* caused a huge explosion below decks and sent it to the bottom. There were just nine survivors.

Eight months before Jutland was the Battle of Loos which would see for the first time in any major action on the Western Front Kitchener's "New Army" of volunteers. Formed

Fine bronze, enhanced by its gold lettering, remembers those that lost their lives. St. John's, Ruardean.

at Bristol in September, 1914, the 10th Gloucestershire Regiment would be in France little more than six weeks before it was thrown into the fighting at Loos on 25 September, 1915. It would be on this day that twenty-one-year-old Private John Thomas Arkell (the second name on the St. John's memorial) would be killed -his battalion having had no more than just a few hours instruction in the trenches, let along any actual battle experience. Going into action at 6.30 am, the 10th Gloucesters suffered their first casualties as gas - British gas - blew back into the lines of the advancing troops. Then the German wire would prove an even greater obstacle than expected - the British barrage prior to the attack having done little to clear a way through for the attackers. For the Bombers that were able to get within a suitable distance from the enemy, it was found that their bombs (hand-grenades), having got wet during the night, in the main failed to explode. All this, together with the severe rifle and machine gun that had swept the Gloucester's ranks since they had left their trenches, would ensure a high casualty rate. Out of a total strength of almost one thousand men, just one hundred and thirty could be accounted for within three days of the battle. Those that had died did so heroically: "The officers fell as the position of their body showed - leading their men, and 16 out of 21 officers were lost. The bodies of our dead now they died with faces to the enemy" (battalion war diary).

Aged twenty-two, Corporal John Edward Bennett Brain was the next to lose his life - this time at Ancora in Turkey on 4 December, 1916 having been wounded and taken prisoner while serving with the Royal Gloucestershire Hussars in Egypt the previous April. This being on St. George's Day (23rd) and during the fighting at Katia.

Serving with the 24th London Regiment when he was killed in France on 25 August, 1917, was forty-two-year-old Private Albert Henry Hale. His battalion being then in the Ypres sector and holding trenches between the Westhoek-Zonnebeke road and the Ypre-Roulers railway.

Just over a year earlier, and on the Somme this time, we find Private Ralph John Howells of the 1/5th Cheshire Regiment. Killed by shell fire on 8 September, 1916 as his battalion went forward to dig a communication tench across a deadly part of the battle area - known as "The Valley of Death" - and up to the recently captured Leuze Wood. Ralph Howells as just eighteen.

We now have Corporal George H. Hussey of the 11th Worcestershire Regiment who died from wounds received in France on 1 August, 1917 - he was thirty-eight - then aged twenty, Private Edward Matthews. One of many from the 1st Herefordshire Regiment to be killed 6 November, 1917 as the regiment went into action at Khuweilfeh, Palestine during the Third Battle of Gaza. "The Herefords on the right, had over-run the flat topped hill but found that they were so enfiladed by machine gun fire that the place was untenable" (Dudley Ward).

Two members of the Meek family follow - Corporal Edward James Meek, another from the 1st Herefords and killed on the same day as his friend Edward Matthews above - then Private Lonal James Meek. Killed on the Somme at Beaumont Hamel as the 11th Border Regiment - on 18 November, 1916 - "....advanced in perfect order to attack. The companies got well away and it is certain that the leading platoons and several others got well over Munich Trench....there was considerable hostile machine-gun fie, apparently from guns well in rear of Frankfort Trench" (battalion war diary).

Others to fall on the Western Front were Lance-Corporal George Stanley Thompson of the 6th Royal Berkshire Regiment (29 March, 1916); Private

Charles Ernest Wheeler, just nineteen when he was killed with the 10th South Wales Borderers on 1 August, 1917 - the battalion experiencing the horrors of Pilckem Ridge on that day - and from the 11th South Wales Borderers, Private Albert Ernest Wilks. Twenty-two when he died from wounds on 22 October, 1918. "Remember o Lord these thy servants and grant unto them eternal rest" - ends the memorial at St. John's.

There are two war graves in the churchyard at St. John's. In the north-west section, another Corporal L.R. Meek of the Herefords (died 2 September, 1917), and also of the Herefords - Private Tom Miles who died 16 December, 1920. He is buried to the north-east of the church. Also in that section, and on a family headstone, is reference to one George Bartlett who "died of wounds" on 1 October, 1917.

ST. BRIAVELS - GLOUCESTERSHIRE

Bounded on the west by the River Wye, St. Briavels lies on the B4228 approximately eight miles north of Chepstow. Entering the village the road becomes Barrowell Lane, then turning left we find at the entrance to playing fields in East Street, a set of gates bearing the dates 1914-1919 and 1939-1945. These being erected as a memorial to those that gave their lives in both world wars.

Simple gates at St. Briavels.

St Mary's

A short distance from the East Street memorial gates is the Parish Church of St. Mary the Virgin. Norman in origin - being restored in 1861 and again in 1882. In the narrow north aisle, old Standards of the St. Briavels and Hewelsfield Branch of the Royal British Legion flank a white marble tablet commemorating those that were killed in the Great War. Names, ranks, regiments, dates and where killed being given for each.

The first man on the memorial, Frederick Trotman, served with the 1st Grenadier Guards and left Southampton with that battalion on 4 October, 1914. Moving forward by road and train, the Guardsmen had reached Ypres by 14 October - afterwards setting up outposts just outside of the town on the Menin and Messines Roads. Here the first enemy - a small cavalry patrol - was seen. The battalion was in action throughout 19 - 26 October, then again on the 29th - that day bringing many casualties as British shells fell short during the morning and the enemy's infantry attacked later in the day.

If travelling up from Chepstow on the A466, you will pass through the Monmouthshire village of Llandogo. Here on the memorial situated on the right of the road is carved the name of Lieutenant Charles Douglas Willoughby Rooke of the 1st Scottish Rifles. The son of a local Justice of the Peace and twenty when he died near the village of Bois Grenier in France, Charles Rooke was hit in three places while out leading a patrol - lying mortally wounded out in no man's land for some time before being brought in.

Corporal Daniel William Trow was originally from Kinley, Shropshire and just eighteen when he lost his life on 9 August, 1915. Less than a week previous, the 9th Worcestershire Regiment had landed at Anzac Cove, Gallipoli and from there moved forward to Aghyl Dere and an attack on the Turkish lines at Hill "Q". In action from 7 pm, 7 August, the battalion fought through until relived three days later - their total casualties being two hundred and sixty-three killed, wounded or missing.

Two men on the St. Briavels memorial died in 1916. Private Theodore Davis of the 1st South African Rifles - during the fighting at Delville Wood on the Somme - followed by Surgeon William Henry Edmunds of the Royal Navy shore establishment HMS *Pembroke*. Twenty-six and the only son of Mr and Mrs J. Edmunds of Brockweir close to Tintern and a few miles south-west of St. Briavels - the memorial gives place of death as Scotland. As far as burial is concerned, the Commonwealth War Graves Commission list two places - Bristol's Greenbank Cemetery and the Kingswood Wesley Methodist Burial Ground (Worcestershire) where he has an "alternative commemoration"?

Neither the records held by the War Office or Commonwealth War Grave Commission list a Private Edward C. Page of the Gloucestershire Regiment having been killed in Salonica - but these do establish the battalion of the next man, Private Reginald J. Stevens, as being 9th Welsh Regiment. John Creswick is unrecorded, Lance-Corporal Victor Butler served with the 2nd Monmouthshire - he was born at Coleford - and Charles Worgan's battalion was 7th Gloucesters. Private Stanley J. Thompson, again nothing found in either Canadian or CWGC records. As the memorial states, Private Frank Dudley of the Yorkshire Regiment (5th Battalion) died in Germany - this being at the age of nineteen and as a prisoner of war. Private William Jellyman Williams, the last name on the memorial and recorded as "missing" 27 May, 1918 can now be confirmed as having died on that date.

An old Standard of the St. Briavels and Hewelsfield Royal British Legion keeps company with the area's war memorials.

Move now to the north side of the churchyard and here on a Commonwealth War Graves Commission headstone bearing the badge of the Gloucestershire Regiment we find the name of Private L.E. Moulton. Thirty-two when he died on 30 October, 1918, and the son of Henry Moulton - gardener to G. Eardley-Wilmot.

ST. DEVEREUX - HEREFORDSHIRE

St. Dubricius

Escaping most maps, St. Devereux lies off the A465 some eight miles south-west of Hereford and within a mile of Kilpeck. Its tiny medieval church - mostly Early English in style (restored 1858, and again 1883) - has a western tower, south porch, chancel and nave. Entering the church, the eye is immediately drawn to the north

Bronze cap badges and coloured enamels at St. Dubricius's Church, St. Devereux.

wall and the war memorial showing various regimental badges and family arms. There are four men from the area (population one hundred and seventy-four in 1911) recorded as having laid down their lives in the Great War.

Their names appearing alongside the badges of the South Wales Borderers and King's (Shropshire Light Infantry), both Charles Watkins and George Young lost their lives while serving with Regular Army battalions during the early months of the war. Having taken part in the Retreat from Mons, the 1st South Wales Borderers later saw action at the Chemin des Dames Ridge (early September) then at Vendresse. When on 26th September the Borderers - holding positions at "The Quarries" on Mont Faucon Ridge - were attacked in great strength and their line overwhelmed, there would be much hand-to-hand fighting. The men picking up any weapon available, one using a table-fork (Atkinson). Private Charles Watkins was one of almost two hundred casualties - mortally wounded and dying four days later.

Just under a month later (23 October), Private George Young (in 1914 a George Young appears in Jackman & Carver's *Directory and Gazetteer of Herefordshire* as a farmer, builder, painter and Assistant Overseer at Revensiege) would died in similar circumstances. The 1st King's (Shropshire Light Infantry) this time, who having first been subject to intense shell fire, were attacked by large numbers of the enemy. Their position being at Bois Grenier.

Both Private Walter Henry Harris and Private Charles Jones served with the Herefordshire Regiment. Walter - his family from Trelough, Wormbridge - was twenty-five when he died on 6 November, 1917, the Herefords in Palestine at that time and in action at Khuweilfeh. Their objective, a dominating hill position important to the progress of the Third Battle of Gaza. Moving steadily forward at 4 pm, the men would reach the reverse slopes of the Khuweilfek Heights, engaging and killing many of the enemy on the way. But before the Herefords could push through to the Turkish main line, a thick mist descended causing confusion among the attackers. Units lost direction, and intermingled, were at one point mistaking and firing upon other regiments thinking that they were the enemy. This, together with heavy machine gun fire and snipers sweeping through the ranks, caused high casualties.

Its services now required on the Western Front, the Herefords embarked at Alexandria for France on 16 June, 1918. Sailing on the transport *Kaiser-l-Hind* and escaping the torpedo (it passed harmlessly astern) of an enemy submarine on the way. Arriving at Taranto, the battalion was on the battlefield by 21 July. Taking over from the French, part of the line facing Bois de Reugny near Posieux. Charles Jones would be killed two days later as his battalion attacked through a field of standing corn - making some one thousand yards, but later brought to a standstill by the intense machine gun fire that swept through the Herefords from the west edge of Bois de Rugny. Total casualties in their first encounter with the enemy in France numbered over two hundred and thirty.

Before leaving St. Dubricius's, take time to visit the grave on the north side of the church of Lance-Corporal Edwin Winstone. Not shown on the memorial (his parents were from Kilpeck) he had served in France with the 1st Monmouthshire Regiment and having returned home suffering from gas poisoning, died of influenza on 28 February, 1919.

ST. WEONARDS - HEREFORDSHIRE

Both the village and its church taking their name from an obscure Welsh saint, St. Weonards lies on the Monmouth to Hereford road (A466). Ten miles south of Hereford, eight miles north of Monmouth, the main road runs through the village less than a mile from the Welsh border. Seen on the skyline for many miles,

St. Weonards west tower is sixteenth century - but much of the church is earlier. The south wall of the nave and chancel arch all dating from c1300. As you enter via the south porch, the eye is immediately drawn to an old Standard of the St. Weonards and District British Legion. This mounted on the central pillar of a fine four-bay arcade separating the north aisle from the nave. Attached to the pillar a small brass plate records the names of six men that fell in the First World War and how, in their memory, the tower clock was erected by fellow parishioners.

The first name on the St. Weonards memorial is that of twenty-four-year-old Lieutenant Ronald Herbert Davis. Son of the Rev. George Herbert Davis and pilot with 48 Squadron, Royal Air Force. The Squadron had been in France since March, 1917 and it would be on 19 August, 1918 that Ronald - in his Bristol F2B aircraft - was in collision with another machine (piloted by Second-Lieutenant E.P. Locke, also of 48 Squadron) west of Peronne and at ten thousand feet. Both aircraft were on an offensive patrol.

The remaining names are those of Thomas Henry Edwards, John and Thomas Harris (John serving with the Canadian Forces), from Vowchurch, William Addis Watkins of the 1st King's Shropshire Light Infantry (killed 13 August, 1918) and George Herbert Williams. Aged twenty-two and one of twenty-one killed on 25 January, 1915 as the 1st South Wales Borderers defended their position at Wagon Hill, Givenchy.

SHIREHAMPTON - GLOUCESTERSHIRE

On the outskirts of Bristol, Shirehampton lies on the Avon to the north-west of the city. Its war memorial being located to the east and on the Shirehampton Road (B4054) close to the golf course. A tall fleury cross, the names of fifty-eight men who died in the First World War are carved into the stonework. The small stone flower-holder at the foot of the cross being presented by the Women's Section of the Shirehampton and District British Legion.

St. Mary's
Drive back into town on the B4054 and Shirehampton Road soon becomes the High Street where St. Mary's is located on the left. The first church stood here from 1844, but this was destroyed by fire on 15 January, 1928. Exactly two years later to the day, the present St. Mary's was opened and installed there in 1930 was a new war memorial in the form of a window featuring Christ on the Cross

surrounded by Roman soldiers. This the gift of the Revd. Clement William Dixon - vicar at St. Mary's 1920-1949 - and bearing the fifty-eight names as shown on the Shirehampton Road memorial. Originally above the altar, the window was removed to its present position over the main entrance at the west end of the church in 1962. Now the parish memorial for both world wars, the names are shown in panels to the left and right of the central light.

Move now into the churchyard and we find two family graves - the headstones of which also commemorate relatives lost while serving overseas. On a Collins family cross we learn that Second-Lieutenant Frank Basil Collins of the 1st South Midland Brigade, Royal Field Artillery was killed in action on 22 August, 1917. The son of George and Mary Collins, he was twenty-four

The gift of its vicar, a window commemorates the dead of both world wars at St. Mary's, Shirehampton.

years old and buried at Vlamertinghe New Military Cemetery in Belgium. The South Midland Artillery, as part of the 48th Division, had, between 16-18 August, 1917, covered the attack at Langemarck north-east of Ypres. An "overwhelming concentration of artillery", notes one record, "such as had never before been approached, not even excepting the Somme". The gunners were also in support on 19 and 22 August as British tanks cleared several enemy strong points.

Mr and Mrs A.J. and L. Mears would lose two sons. Details of which appear at the base of another cross in the churchyard accompanied by loving words. On one side the name of thirty-one year old Thomas Henry Mears, killed in action on 7 April, 1917, is followed by: "And Now He Is Sleeping His Last Long Sleep And His Grave I May Never See. But Some Gentle Hand In The Distant Land May Scatter Some Flowers For Me." Sergeant Mears of the 2/4th Gloucestershire Regiment is buried in Chapelle British Cemetery at Holnon, France and was killed shortly after his battalion took over trenches west of Fresnoy on 6 April. The Gloucesters that same evening attacking the village and consolidating its gains throughout the night. On 7 August, the date of Tom's death, the battalion war diary records snow and a very cold, but "quiet" day. Casualties numbered one killed and one missing.

Tom's younger brother Private Eli Ernest was twenty-seven and his family recall: "When Last We Saw His Smiling Face He Looked So Strong And Brave. Little We Thought How Soon He'd Be Laid In A Hero's Grave." Buried at Grande-Seraucourt British Cemetery south-west of St. Quentin on the east side of the River Somme, he had served with "A" Company of the 2/5th Gloucestershire Regiment and died from wounds received on 26 March, 1917. Turning to Captain A.F. Barnes, MC, and his history of the 2/5th Gloucestershire Regiment, we read how the period from 21 March, 1917 "....was the most critical one that the Glosters ever went through." He notes in particular the night of the 22nd which "....will abide for ever in the minds of those who were privileged to live through it." The 2/5th at the time in question had played an important role in holding up three German divisions - this contributing to the successful crossing of the Somme by the 5th Army.

STAUNTON - GLOUCESTERSHIRE

All Saints

On the A4136 three miles east of Monmouth, Staunton lies on high ground overlooking the Valley of the Wye. The embattled central tower of its church being clearly seen as you approach the village. Late Norman (it was restored in 1872) All Saints has just one fine war memorial. On the wall of the north aisle and beautiful decorated in blues, reds and gold, it features Christ on the Cross and takes the form of a triptych - the doors of which carry the dedication. There are just two names, William Ebborn Ambury, William Edmund Barnett, and these are seen within a gold framed panel below the Crucifix. William Edmund Barnett is also commemorated on the headstone of a family grave south of the church.

Also south of the church is another family grave recording the death of a son. This time that of Bede Liddell Fenton of the 1st Dorsetshire Regiment. On the first day of the Battle of the Somme (1st July, 1916) the 1st Dorsetshire suffered some five hundred casualties - most of which occurred in the early part of the day and during the battalion's move forward from assembly positions in Authuille Wood to the British front line. In the firing line again on 8 July, this time in the Ovillers

Two men from Staunton that could not be remembered better than by this fine memorial at All Saints.

sector, the trenches were so congested with dead and wounded (battalion war diary) that one company under Captain Fenton was sent back into the support line. On 15 July, however, and at 2.50 am, he led a small raiding party against two enemy points - this operation being unsuccessful and costing him his life. Thirty-three-year-old Captain Fenton was the son of the Rev. E. and Mrs Margaret Fenton.

THRUXTON - HEREFORDSHIRE

St. Bartholomew's

Just six miles south-west of Hereford, on the Ross to Hay-on-Wye road (B4348), the small parish of Thruxton (population 69 in 1911) has three names on its war memorial. This to be seen on the north wall at St. Bartholomew's. Mostly fourteenth century and comprising chancel, nave, a timber south porch and Early-English west tower.

A brass tablet mounted on wood, the names are surmounted by a crown and two flags. Little is known of Sergeant Mark Jones who, killed in Belgium on 15 December, 1917, must have emigrated before the war. Serving as he did with the 1st Canterbury Regiment, New Zealand Expeditionary Force. First in Egypt, the regiment, in April, 1916 moved to France and there took part in the September-October operations on the Somme - Flers-Courcelette, Morval and Le Transloy. The Battle of Messines followed in June, 1917, then having moved to the Ypres Salient the Canterbury Regiment saw action at Polygon Wood, Broodseind and Passchendaele. Mark Jones, who was twenty-six, is buried in the Menin Road South Military Cemetery just east of Ypres.

As Pioneer battalion to the 13th (Western) Division, the 8th Welsh Regiment left Aldershot for Avonmouth on 15 June, 1915 - destination the Dardanelles. Arriving at Lemnos in the Ægean Sea, the battalion for the time being was put to work on road-building and the construction of a jetty. This important island acting as a military base for operations on Gallipoli. Having crossed to the Peninsular, the Pioneers later saw front line service in the Anzac sector, and at Suvla where there would be more construction work. Evacuated from Gallipoli on 16 December, Egypt came next, then from there (in February, 1916) Mesopotamia. Here the battalion took part in the capture of Hanna and Fallahiya, followed by the subsequent operations at Sanniyat. Baghdad was occupied on 11 March, 1917 - the Pioneers taking an active part in its subsequent consolidation.

The 12th Welsh Regiment, the battalion recorded along with Thomas John Parry's name, was a reserve unit from which he would have been transferred. Born at Edgbaston, Warwickshire, he resided at Allensmore (west of Thruxton) and was aged thirty-six when he died on 10 July, 1917.

Also to die in Mesopotamia (25 April, 1916) was Private James Hazlewood of the 1st Manchester Regiment. Born at Northampton, Pennsylvania, USA (records the War Office). It was while resident in the Thruxton area that he enlisted into the Army at Hereford. Receiving orders to leave for an "unknown destination" the Manchesters left France on 11 December, 1915. Travelling on the *Huntsend* - a captured German liner (*Lützow*) - the battalion steamed eastwards, and by 6 January, 1916 were just off Koweit. Here the troops learnt that they were destined for Mesopotamia where extensive efforts were to be made to relieve General Townsend's force at Kut.

From Basra, the Manchesters covered the last part of their journey forward by barge - moving slowly up the Shatt-el-Arab to camp at Shaik Sa'ad. Reached on

18 January, this position had recently been captured from the Turks who were now holding strongly defended positions at Hannah. For the next weeks - the troops spending most of their time holding trenches close to the Tigris - the battalion records note casualties as "light" (two killed, three wounded). But this would change when on 8 March a strong attack was made at Dujailah Redoubt. A heavily fortified position situated between the Tigris and Shatt-el-Hai.

Going forward at 5.15 pm., the Manchesters, on a front of four hundred yards, directed the advance. Turkish guns firing from the Sinn Aftar Redoubt enfilading the attackers as they came on. But, wrote one eyewitness "....they were steady as a machine, and did not stop to pick up their wounded or dying." Two enemy lines occupied by 5.20, the Manchesters began clearing the area - but soon a heavy counter-attack developed, and, as fire from the flanks increased, the battalion was ordered to withdraw. All ground gained being abandoned by dusk. Total casualties (records Colonel H.C. Wylly in his history of the Manchester Regiment) amounting to four hundred and sixty killed, wounded of missing.

Further casualties by the 1st Manchester Regiment (period 4 - 18 April) totalled seven killed, thirty-two wounded and one missing. James Hazlewood is buried in the Baghdad (North Gate) War Cemetery, Iraq.

TIDENHAM - GLOUCESTERSHIRE

St. Mary's
On a peninsular formed by the Severn and Wye, St. Mary's, Tidenham lies just outside Chepstow on the A48 - its medieval west tower serving as a navigational landmark to sailors on the Severn through many centuries.

Erected by the parishioners of both Tidenham and Beachley - Beachley to the south and where the old Severn road bridge crosses - the memorial at St. Mary's will be found on the north aisle. In marble it records the names of thirty-five who gave their lives. There is also an illuminated Roll of Honour listing in fine handwriting the names of the two hundred and twenty-seven that served in the forces during the war.

TWIGWORTH - GLOUCESTERSHIRE

St. Matthew's

Built 1842-4 by Thomas Fulljames, Twigworth's church lies at the side of the main Tewkesbury road (A35) just to the north of Gloucester. "Elegant yet prim" (Verey), St. Matthew's has chancel, nave of four bays, a north aisle, western tower with high spire, and within its churchyard the parish war memorial. A Calvary cross on the base of which are inscribed the names of fifteen dead from the Great War.

Before entering St. Matthew's, walk from the memorial to the north side of the church. Here you will find the grave of Gloucester poet, musician, songwriter and soldier of the First World War, Ivor Bertie Gurney. Serving with the 2/5th Gloucestershire Regiment on the western front, where he was both

Ivor Gurney - "A Lover and Maker of Beauty" - his original headstone now inside the church at Twigworth.

wounded and gassed, he would survive the war. But its horrors could not be removed from his mind and after twenty years of pain and torment he would end his life in a lunatic asylum in 1937.

But the headstone seen here today is not the original. Made from a local soft stone and in the form of a Celtic Cross, by 1990 (one hundred years after his birth) the inscription on the first monument had become weathered. Being re-cut that year - only to be vandalised on New Year's Eve seven years later. Repaired, it stood in place for a few more years, but in 2001 the decision was taken to remove the headstone to a place of safety within the church. At time of writing (August, 2002) it stands in the north aisle - soon to be the centre-piece of an exhibition.

Move to the east side of the churchyard now and here, with Commonwealth War Graves Commission headstones are the graves of five First World War

Soldiers: Ordinary-Seaman S.F. Bond, Royal Naval Volunteer Reserve and just seventeen when he died on 9 October, 1918; Private H. Dalley, 16th Worcestershire Regiment, 15 May, 1920; Private A.E. Halford, 3rd Gloucestershire Regiment, 16 May, 1919; Private Thomas Henry Hawkins, Labour Corps, 7 April, 1921 and Sergeant Ernest Aubry Kemp of the 1st Battalion, Grenadier Guards, died 28 March, 1919.

The church remembers another member of the 2/5th Gloucesters on the wall of the north aisle. Corporal Arthur Beak who, having been wounded in France on 21 June, 1916 - the battalion in trenches at Fauquissart at this time - was later sent to hospital at Cambridge. He subsequently died on 8 October and was buried, along with one hundred and eighty-one other First World War servicemen, in Cambridge City Cemetery.

Before leaving St. Matthew's note two items of interest. A memorial to a soldier of the Crimea War who fell during the Charge of the Light Brigade, and the church piano. Just an ordinary Edwardian upright, but that on which Ivor Gurney played during his association at Twigworth with Canon Alfred Hunter Cheesman.

VOWCHURCH - HEREFORDSHIRE

St. Bartholomew's

In Herefordshire's Golden Valley, Vowchurch lies off the B4348 approximately halfway between Hereford and Hay-on-Wye. A short drive off the main road taking you down to St. Bartholomew's where on the edge of the River Dore, part of its south wall is Norman. But it is from the fourteenth century that most of the church dates. Inside, and between Jacobean oak woodwork, the parish war memorial is situated on the north wall of the nave - a brass plaque and recording five names without rank or regiment.

William Barrell was born at Pontrilas and as a Private with "B" Company, 1st South Wales Borderers, died from wounds received in France on 27 September, 1915. There are two Seabornes (William and Edgar) - the latter, who with the 7th King's Shropshire Light Infantry, died on the Somme (13 November, 1916). Jakeman & Carver's *Directory and Gazetteer of Herefordshire* for 1914 records members of this family as farmers and a stone mason. Of Slate Cottage, and the son of Charles and Matilda, Private Charles Skyrme was nineteen when he succumbed to his wounds on 29 March, 1918. His battalion, the 4th Royal Fusiliers, being at that time holding trenches in the Cherisy Fountaine sector, France.

The last name on the memorial at St. Bartholomew's is that of Private Ernest Thomas. Killed in action on the Somme (30 August, 1916) and from Holsty Farm just east of Vowchurch. He served with the 6th King's Shropshire Light Infantry and has no know grave.

WALFORD-ON-WYE - HEREFORDSHIRE

St. Michael and All Angels

At Walford, close to the Wye and just below Ross, its church provides "value for money" in its collection of war memorials. Starting as they do literally at the beginning of the lane leading up to its entrance, carrying on up through the lychgate, within the churchyard and throughout the church itself. First, and greeting us as we arrive, a fine monument by Gilbert Boulton of Grosvenor Studios, Cheltenham, forms the first of two parish memorials. This a tall pillar in the front of which stands the figure of St. George. At his feet, and carved into two stone tablets, the twenty-four names of those that died "For King and Country".

As you begin walking up the path you are now *in* Walford's second memorial - the "Avenue of Remembrance" with its lime trees planted in 1923. A slab of local stone placed at the end, and to the left of the lychgate, tells the story: "The avenue lining the approach to the church commemorates those men of the village who fell in the 1914-1918 war. A tree was planted for each life given. Each man is named on the war memorial at the church main gate. We will remember them."

At the foot of each tree a small rectangle of stone was placed bearing the name of a single soldier, along with date and place of his death ("St. Eloe" - "Sulva Bay" - "At Sea" - "Ypres" - "Gommecourt" - "Arass" - "Alexandria" - "Cambrai" - "Marne" and others from all theatres of war). The stones we see today though are recent replacements - but many of the originals, now worn, broken and discarded in the undergrowth - remain still.

Through the lychgate now (this also a memorial, but to those killed 1939-1945) then into the churchyard. First the Commonwealth War Graves Commission headstones marking the graves of three soldiers - on the west side Private John Morgan of the 2nd King's (Shropshire Light Infantry), twenty-six when he died on 25 May, 1915 and from the Herefordshire Regiment, Private Harold Ernest Huntly Evans, 10 June, 1920. On the south side of the churchyard we have the grave of nineteen-year-old Private Kenneth Percival Stevens Bevan who served with the 6th KSLI and lived at Whitings Lane, Walford.

Look now for three family graves that also commemorate relatives lost and buried overseas. West of the church and on a headstone belonging to Winifred Sarah Hawker of Hill Court Gardens, we see reference to her brother, Sergeant Arthur Allen Hawker who was killed in action on 9 September, 1918. He served with No. 1 Company, 4th Battalion, Grenadier Guards and St. Michael's has plaque (to the left of the door on the north side) to his memory - placed there by his father and mother in 1924.

Also on the west side a cross marking the graves of several members of the Butt family tells how two brother died elsewhere - Richard Acton and Frederick Claude Butt - eldest and youngest sons of G.W. and E.S. Butt of Holcombe. More of them inside the church. Near the lychgate see on another headstone reference to Harold William Symonds. Killed on the Marne 30 May, 1918.

St. George greets us at the beginning of Walford's "Avenue of Remembrance".

The church guide tells how St. Michael's was once dedicated to St. Leonard (the name changing at the restoration of the building in 1887) and how the church is one of the earliest in Herefordshire - the centre part of its nave being built c1100. But the church is essentially thirteenth century, the tower being added then and at first standing alone and topped by a spire. This being struck during a thunderstorm in February, 1813 and falling to the ground.

Remember the Butt brothers from the churchyard? - well at the west end of the church you will find a fine window to their memory. Below St. David and St. Jonathan, two angels hold a scroll bearing the dedication which tells how the boys "....were lovely and pleasant in their lives and in death they were not divided." Then below this a marble tablet bears the devices of two regiments - the King's Shropshire Light Infantry and the London Rifle Brigade.

A Second-Lieutenant attached to 5th KSLI, Richard Butt, who having reported for duty while the battalion was in billets at Houtkerque, was killed within days of his arrival on 9 January. The tablet noting that he was twenty-four and buried at Brielin. Turning now to his brother, we learn from the memorial that Frederick was taken prisoner at Gommecourt on 1 July, 1916. On this, the first day of the Battle of the Somme, the London Rifle Brigade, with other units from the 56th (1st London) Division, suffered heavy losses. Its strength when going into battle shortly after 7.30 am being over eight hundred – upon returning to the British lines at 5 pm, just eighty-nine unwounded men were counted. It would appear that his burial six days after he was captured, was by the Germans.

Turn now to face the church's fine north door - to the left, a small brass plaque belonging to the Sergeant Arthur Allen Hawker that we saw mentioned on his sister's headstone in

A brother, killed in action in France, shares a headstone inscription with his sister. St. Michael and All Angels churchyard, Walford.

the churchyard - and on the right another memorial. This time a bronze plaque, mounted on wood and displaying a family crest, recalling the death at Georgetown, Demerara, British Guiana, of one Lionel Beale Kyrle Collins in 1894. But it is the name below that is of First World War interest; Lionel Drummond Kyrle Collins, Second-Lieutenant, 3rd (attached to 13th) Battalion, Royal Scots - killed in action on 12 May, 1916 aged twenty-two.

The 13th Royal Scots were holding trenches facing the heavily defended German position known as the Hohenzollern Redoubt in the Loos sector. "The enemy's success", notes the historian of the Royal Scots, Major John Ewing, MC, "had given him a firmer grip on the Hohenzollern Redoubt, which had been a veritable cockpit ever since the 25th September 1915. Mining, counter-mining, and infantry clashes were almost a matter of daily routine...." It was one such "infantry clash" that led up to Lionel Collins's death. On the day before, then enemy, after a terrific bombardment of the Royal Scots trenches, attacked and succeeded in entering part of their front line. Subsequent attempts to penetrate deeper, and into the support and reserve trenches, were all repelled "....heavy rifle and Lewis gun fire was poured into the Boches, inflicting on them many casualties."

But the battalion's losses had to be reclaimed, and at 1.30 am on 12 May, the Royal Scots charged across open land – "....but the Boches were ready for this move and shattered the assault by the accuracy of their fire. Total losses amounted to more than two hundred and thirty killed, wounded or missing. Lionel Collins being one of the latter.

The last memorial at St. Michael's will be found in the chancel where to the left of the altar a brass missal stand recalls the death near Yores on 19 August, 1917 of twenty-two-year-old Colin Eric Baumgarte. A lance-corporal serving with the 2/8th Worcestershire Regiment, he was killed by shell fire as that battalion occupied positions running from Pommern Castle to Spree Farm. The stand was presented to the church by his mother Annie Baumgarte.

WESTBURY-ON-SEVERN – GLOUCESTERSHIRE

The detached tower at St. Mary, St. Peter and St. Paul's, on the A48 nine miles south-west of Gloucester, dates from c1270 (originally a garrison or watch-tower notes Verey) and lies some fifty feet from the church itself. This being no earlier than c1300.

Outside the church, and erected "To the glory of God and in grateful memory of the men of Westbury parish who gave their lives for their king and country in the Great War" is the village war memorial. A tall shaft

War graves at St. Mary, St. Peter and St. Paul's, Westbury-on-Severn.

with a carved stone calvary set back into a recess at the side of the road. The names of the dead are seen on the bronze panels either side.

Before entering the church look around the churchyard for the Commonwealth War Graves Commission headstones belonging to the three First World War soldiers buried on its north side – Private Alfred Arthur Trott (13th Somerset Light Infantry, died 13 December, 1918), Private A.J. Warren (5th Gloucestershire Regiment, 28 April, 1918) and Driver Maurice Wintle (Royal Engineers, 5 March, 1915).

Inside now and their names, with thirty-seven others, appear again. This time on an illuminated Roll of Honour hanging from the wall of the north aisle.

Westbury's tall memorial cross on the roadside close to St. Mary, St. Peter and St. Paul's.

YORKLEY

On the southern edge of the Forest of Dean, Yorkley lies approximately three miles north of Lydney and can be reached via the B4234. Surrounded by a low railing, the village war memorial is located in the recreational area on Bailey Hill. At the base of the column, this taking the form of a four-columned temple, a short dedication carved into the front panel reads: "Erected to the honour and memory of the above men who fell in the Great War 1914-1919." Above this, and placed around four sides (one word on each) are the words "Honour", "Sacrifice", "Valour" and "Courage". The names of those that fell appear in no particular order on the shaft of the column below a laurel wreath.

BIBLIOGRAPHY

Much of the information included – that dealing with village and church history – has been taken from those good old reference tools produced by Pevsner (*The Buildings of England)*, Mee *(The King's England)* and Kelly *(Directories)* (see below), but of tremendous value have been the lovingly prepared (too many to list) guide books and short histories that are available at the churches themselves. As for military and regimental information, this too has come from a number of essential sources – *Soldiers Died in the Great War* and the meticulously kept records of the Commonwealth War Graves Commission being two of those most widely used. Certain regimental and unit histories have also been important and these have been listed below. Other lesser used volumes have been mentioned within the text. On the unpublished side, probably the most important reference source here would be the unit war diary. Written, more or less, "in the field" and, in my view, an essential tool regarding any form of regimental history. These are available in their original form at the Public Records Office, but this author is lucky in as much as these "worth their weight in gold" documents exist (in photocopy form) in his own collection of military records (another important information source) – the "Ray Westlake Unit Archives".

Barnett, Lieutenant-Colonel George Henry, CMG, DSO. 1923. *With the 48th Division in Italy.* Edinburgh and London: William Blackwood and Sons.

Dudley Ward, DSO, MC, Major C.H. 1927. *History of the 53rd (Welsh) Division (T.F.) 1914-1918.* Cardiff: Western Mail Ltd.

Fox, Frank. 1923. *The History of the Royal Gloucestershire Hussars Yeomanry 1898-1922.* London: Philip Allan & Co.

Holt, Captain H.P. 1937. *The History of the Third (Prince of Wales's) Dragoon Guards, 1914-1918.* Guildford: Billing and Sons Ltd.

Leonard, John. 2000. *Churches of Herefordshire & their Treasures.* Logaston: Logaston Press.

Mee, Arthur. 1940. *The King's England - Gloucestershire.* London: Hodder and Stoughton.

Mee, Arthur. 1938. *The King's England - Herefordshire.* London: Hodder and Stoughton.

Pevsner, Nikolaus. 1963. *The Buildings of England - Herefordshire.* London: Penguin Books.

Salter, Mike. *The Old Parish Churches of Herefordshire.* Folly Publications.

Verey, David (Nikolaus Pevsner ed.). 1970. *The Buildings of England, Gloucestershire: The Vale and The Forest of Dean.* Harmondsworth: Penguin Books.

Westlake, Ray. 1994. *British Battalions on the Somme.* Barnsley: Leo Cooper, Pen & Sword Books Ltd.

Westlake, Ray. 1996. *British Regiments at Gallipoli.* Barnsley: Leo Cooper, Pen & Sword Books Ltd.

Westlake, Ray. 1997. *British Battalions in France & Belgium 1914.* Barnsley: Leo Cooper, Pen & Sword Books Ltd.

Westlake, Ray. 2001. *British Battalions on the Western Front January to June 1915.* Barnsley: Leo Cooper, Pen & Sword Books Ltd.

Wyrall, Everard. 1931. *The Gloucestershire Regiment in the Great War 1914-1918.* London: Methuen & Co. Ltd.

INDEX